SEEDS OF PROGRESS

TO *Stewart L. Long*

*The one who tries freedom—
the sower of seeds and the
beneficiary of progress.*

All my best!

OTHER BOOKS BY LEONARD E. READ

Romance of Reality (o.p.)
Pattern for Revolt
Instead of Violence
Outlook for Freedom (o.p.)
Government: An Ideal Concept
  Governo Um Concito Ideal
Why Not Try Freedom?
  ¿Por Que No Ensayar la Libertad?
Elements of Libertarian Leadership
Anything That's Peaceful
  Todo Por la Paz
The Free Market and Its Enemy
  El Enemigo del Mercado Libre
Deeper Than You Think
Accent on the Right
The Coming Aristocracy
Let Freedom Reign
Talking to Myself
Then Truth Will Out
To Free or Freeze
Who's Listening?
Having My Way
Castles In The Air
The Love of Liberty
Comes the Dawn
Awake for Freedom's Sake
Vision
Liberty: Legacy of Truth
The Freedom Freeway

LEONARD E. READ

SEEDS OF PROGRESS

The Foundation for Economic Education, Inc.
Irvington-on-Hudson, New York 10533
1980

THE AUTHOR AND PUBLISHER

Leonard E. Read has been president of The Foundation for Economic Education since it was organized in 1946.

The Foundation is a nonpolitical, nonprofit, educational institution. Its senior staff and numerous writers are students as well as teachers of the free market, private ownership, limited government rationale. Sample copies of the Foundation's monthly study journal, *The Freeman*, are available on request.

Published March 1980

ISBN-0-910614-65-2 (cloth)
ISBN-0-910614-66-0 (paper)

Copyright © 1980 by Leonard E. Read

Permission to reprint granted without special request.

Printed in U.S.A.

CONTENTS

1. LITTLE THINGS: THE SEEDS OF
   PROGRESS   1

   Progress springs from countless individual crea-
   tivities freely flowing.

2. POLITICAL BUNGLING   9

   Men are strangely inclined to worship what they
   do not understand.

3. TWO WAYS TO GO WRONG   14

   The planned chaos of socialism and the unplanned chaos of anarchy.

4. THE PRETENDER'S PLAGUE   21

   Beware of those who pretend to be what they
   are not.

5. POLITICAL STEALING   26

   The seekers of loot share the sins of the political looters.

6. LIVING: BY ROTE OR BY WHAT'S RIGHT 30

   To avoid vain repetitions, explore the righteous.

7. AUTHORITY: TO BE EMBRACED OR REJECTED? 35

   Authority intoxicates and makes sots of magistrates.

8. GOOD DOERS OR DO-GOODERS? 41

   Do-gooders can hold no power over good-doers.

9. FICKLE CONTRADICTIONS 46

   Virtuous tyrants—a contradiction in terms—spur us to resist and overcome.

10. "ABOUT FACE": REFORMERS! 51

    To be informed is the best defense against reformers.

11. FLOWERS: EMBLEMS OF HUMAN FLOWERING 55

    "We are shaped and fashioned by what we love." Let us love freedom.

12. THE BLESSINGS OF MORAL OBLIGATIONS 59

    Our blessings are measurable in their power to improve us.

Contents

13. TWIN VIRTUES: RESPONSIBLE AND RESPONSIVE 64

    Man does not fall into freedom but must raise himself to it.

14. TO ACQUIRE? DESIRE AND ASPIRE! 69

    Grant that I may always desire more than I can accomplish.

15. BELIEVE IN THIS MIRACLE: FREEDOM 75

    Believe in our miracle and freedom will rise again.

16. THE GLORY OF OUR WORLDS GALORE 80

    May our duties be well performed and all our days well spent.

17. THE SOURCE OF WISDOM 85

    Wisdom consists of discovering and abiding by the good.

18. THE KEYS TO GREATNESS 89

    Coming to one's purpose involves overcoming obstacles.

19. LIVING THE GOOD LIFE 94

    Forgo denunciation of freedom's opponents. Leave them nothing to scratch against.

20. INFLUENCE: ITS ETERNAL RADIATION 99

Let him who would improve the world first improve himself.

21. FINDING ONE'S DUTY 104

We are not born to solve the problems of the Universe.

22. SO HIGHLY ENDOWED 110

The guaranteed life turns out to be not only not free—it's not safe!

23. TOWARD THE IDEAL 114

The path toward freedom is an endless succession of ideas.

24. AS A MAN THINKETH 119

From the active mind comes achievement and production.

25. THE POWER OF TOMORROW 124

The future depends upon our present performances.

INDEX 127

1
LITTLE THINGS: THE SEEDS OF PROGRESS

> *The greatest things ever done on earth have been done by little and little—little agents, little persons, little things, by every one doing his own work, filling his own sphere, holding his own post, and saying, "Lord, what will thou have me to do?"* —**THOMAS GUTHRIE**

The above, by this Scottish divine (1803-78), suggests that he may have learned a great deal from his Scottish predecessor, the remarkable Adam Smith (1723-90), for there is a striking similarity in their thinking.

The mass of citizens who haven't the slightest idea of what makes an economy fruitful or unfruitful, perform trillions of little things that result in an abundance of goods and services beneficial to millions of others whom they have no conscious intention of benefiting. If these benefactors are not guided by politico-economic understanding, what then? Adam Smith wrote an answer 200 years ago: "By directing that industry in such a manner as its produce may be of the greatest value, he intends only his own gain, and he is in this, as in many other cases, led by an invisible hand to promote an end which was no part of his intention."

The common cause Adam Smith and Thomas Guthrie identified is intelligent self-interest: "Lord, what will thou have me to do?"

Adam Smith's "invisible hand" is probably what Guthrie meant by "Lord"—Infinite Consciousness or Creation, the nondimensional, having no boundaries, that which cannot even be imagined by finite mortals. However, if we are to understand the little things by which we live and prosper, we must recognize that this Infinity is their source. The late Donald Hatch Andrews, among the greatest of scientists, gave this truth an excellent phrasing in his book, *The Symphony of Life:* "I suggest that we postulate that the intangibles of truth and beauty, *human freedom*, courage, honor, honesty are the core of the truly basic realities; and that the supposed realities which we see and touch and feel [little things] *are really only shadows cast by these truly basic dynamic forms.*"

Were none of us to grasp this point, namely, that the little things are but the shadows of Divine Omniscience, requiring the practice of moral principles, there would be no great things. Live the righteous life or perish!

Americans came nearer to living the righteous life than the people of any other nation. Result? The greatest prosperity ever known—more little things than ever before in history! Affluence, however, has its dangers. As Horace, the Roman of 2,000 years ago, stated: "Adversity has the effect of eliciting talents which in times of prosperity would have lain dormant."

Why does affluence lead to the loss of freedom? When people are graced with countless millions of little things the loss of one or two or thousands is negligible compared to the total, and is shrugged off as meaningless. "Observe how prosperous we are!" The source of their well-being—living by moral principles—is mostly forgotten. Uncorrected, this leads to adversity.

Reflect on the situation in primitive societies living a hand-to-mouth existence. The "little things" are few and far between, each one vital to survival. The loss of a single one would be a calamity. And calamities are talking alarm clocks: "Wake up! Come to yourselves! Examine the causes of your plight!"

There's no doubt in my mind that the greatest cause of our own plight stems from dismissing Creation as the source of human felicity and placing finite man in that role. It is important that we see the utter fallacy of this role reversal. Nor need we look to morons as the authors of such balderdash. More often than not it originates with those who are among the wisest in their own fields. Plato and Dr. Alexis Carrel should suffice as examples.

Life in Athens of twenty-four centuries ago was relatively simple. Economics as a discipline had not been considered; technology as we know it was nonexistent; specialization in medicine, manufacturing, or in any other field had scarcely begun. Computers? Why, even the concept of zero was a thousand years in the future. Athenians, by our standards, knew nothing of the complexities we experience in everyday life.

Simple? In a sense, yes. Yet, human beings were as complex then as now. Each individual was unique. No two thought alike, or had the same incentives, talents, desires, likes, dislikes, goals, energies. Variation! And to the mind of a social planner this spelled chaos, humanity at sixes and sevens. How possibly could order be brought out of such disorder? Precisely the same question people raise today. And inspired by the same lack of understanding!

Plato gave us the philosopher-king idea—an omnipotent leader wise enough to play a totally dominant role. Plato's final statement of this absurd idea is found in *Laws* Book 12, #942, where he has the Athenian say:

> The greatest principle of all is that nobody, whether male or female, should be without a leader. Nor should the mind of anybody be habituated to letting him do anything at all on his own initiative; neither out of zeal, nor even playfully. But in war as in the midst of peace—to his leader he shall direct his eye and follow him faithfully. And even in the smallest matter he should stand under leadership. For example, he should get up, or move, or wash, or take his meals . . . only if he has been told to do so. In a word, he should teach his soul, by long habit, never to dream of acting independently, and to become utterly incapable of it.

Was the above Plato's idea of the way a "leader" should run our lives or was he trying to show the absurdity of such dictatorship by ever so many others? I have no way of knowing but many others, brilliant in their own fields, have taken this identical position. For an example, read *Man, The Unknown* by a distinguished scientist, Dr. Alexis Carrel.[1]

Most of this book is devoted to a skillful and critical analysis of our decline into the planned economy and the welfare state—Socialism. After enumerating ever so many advanced specializations Carrel claims that no one has all

---
[1] See *Man, The Unknown* (New York: Harper & Brothers), 1935.

Seeds of Progress

such knowledge in his possession. Of course no one does but Dr. Carrel believes a few *should* possess it all. Reflect on his solution:

> In about twenty-five years of uninterrupted study, one could learn these sciences. At the age of fifty, those who have submitted themselves to this discipline could effectively *direct* the construction of the human being and of a civilization. . . .
>
> We have to *intervene* in the fundamental organic and mental processes. These processes are man himself. But man has no independent existence. He is bound to his environment. In order to *remake* him, we have to transform his world. . . .
>
> A group, although very small, is capable of eluding the harmful influence of the society of its epoch by *imposing* upon its members rules of conduct modeled on *military* or monastic discipline. . . .
>
> Such a minority would be in a position to impose by persuasion or perhaps *by force*, other ways of life upon the majority. . . .
>
> We must single out the children who are endowed with high potentialities, and develop them as completely as possible. . . .

Who are "we"? It's a million-to-one bet that "we" would never have singled out that 12-year-old newsboy in Michigan—Thomas Alva Edison.

> The sons of very rich men, like those of criminals, should be removed while still infants from their natural surroundings.

Peacefully? Hardly! The removal would have to be at the point of a gun; rich parents love their children, too!

C. S. Lewis had this to say about those of the Philosopher King school: "I am not supposing them to be bad men. They are, rather, not men (in the old sense) at all. They are, if you like, men who have sacrificed their own share in traditional humanity in order to devote themselves to the task of deciding what 'Humanity' shall henceforth mean."

The mere acceptance of the lording-it-over-man concept paves the way for coercionists or war lords. Some people are drawn to the idea of a Leader who has synthesized all knowledge. They search in vain, for no such person exists. Frustrated they exalt government into a Philosopher King. No need to mention names. The 16,000,000 officials in our 78,000 governments—federal, state and local—who believe they can run our lives better than we can, discouragingly approach 99 per cent. They step out of bounds, as we say; they go over and beyond the role intended for man; they step into God's Realm and fall into an abyss of utter absurdity.

Plato, when young, may or may not have been a Philosopher King advocate. In any event, as he grew older, he devoted his best efforts to the *erection of barriers* to the exercise of coercive power of one human over another.

The mind that can combine all knowledge or any tiny part thereof is not to be found among our kind. There is only one: the CREATOR! I have never heard anyone contradict Joyce Kilmer's "Only God can make a tree." If man cannot make even a tree, how can one logically contend that man can make or remake man? Surely, man is higher in Creation's Design than a tree!

The Philosopher King syndrome, on the rampage, is causing countless adversities—calamities. As noted before, these are talking alarm clocks: "Wake up! Come to yourselves! Examine the causes of your plight!"

In what manner do these errors elicit talents that because of our prosperity have been lying dormant? Plutarch, the Greek essayist and biographer of 19 centuries ago, gave to posterity an excellent answer: "To make no mistakes is not in the power of man; but from their errors and mistakes the wise and good learn wisdom for the future."

What are the wise and good learning?

- That intelligent self-interest, minding one's own business, is the limited role of man.
- That truth and beauty, human freedom, courage, honor, honesty are the core of the truly basic realities.
- That the realities which we see and touch—our material blessings—are really only shadows cast by an adherence to heavenly principles—what the Lord, not dictocrats, would have us do.
- That each of us should do our little creative things and let everyone else—no exceptions—do theirs. These trillions times trillions of little things are, indeed, the seeds of all human progress and are founded on liberty for one and all.

As to liberty, hear ye this (James 1:25): "But whosoever looketh into the perfect law of liberty, and continueth therein, he being not a forgetful hearer, but a doer of the work, this man shall be blessed in his deed."

May more and more men and women strive to be such exemplars!

***

Lord, what will thou have me do? The answer: Pursue that goal which harmonizes with your highest *creative* aspiration. Mine happens to be finding ways to explain the fallacies of socialism and the truths of freedom.

Thank heaven that others have aspirations that differ and come first with them: for example, the production and exchange of countless goods and services by which we survive and prosper. Were all aspirations identical to mine, we would perish. Yet, if mine—freedom—were to cease as a way of life, adversity would predominate and human evolution would cease.

The following chapters in this, my 26th book, pursue the same subject as previous books, only the phrasing differs. Why the variation? One mode of speech is understood by a few, another by a different few.

One aspiration you might share with me: advance freedom by an improved phrasing of its truths.

2
POLITICAL BUNGLING

I hate all bungling as I do sin, but particularly bungling in politics, which leads to the misery and ruin of many thousands and millions of people. **—GOETHE**

What is a bungler? "A clumsy, awkward workman." Briefly, he is one so lacking in grace and skill that he acts ineptly and irresponsibly. In what occupational category are bunglers most numerous? Politicians—elected and appointed!

To dramatize the point of this thesis, imagine this fictitious situation—the firemen of a community answering an alarm and rushing to a burning home. Failing to extinguish the fire immediately, they spray the home with kerosene. The fire worsens. The remedy? Spray it with gasoline! Still worse! On and on with "remedies" galore, each more moronic than the former. These imaginary firemen resemble the millions of political bunglers whose actions lead to "the misery and ruin of many thousands and millions of people."

The English novelist, Henry Fielding, might well have referred to political bungling when he observed: "Men are strangely inclined to worship what they do not understand."

Let us not be too severe in charging that the political bunglers have deserted the freedom way of life. No one can desert or abandon a faith never held! On the subject of freedom, the political bunglers have drawn blanks. An honest confession: I have drawn a blank on many thousands of subjects. And who hasn't!

Most people are unaware—have drawn a blank—as to how the free, unfettered flow of ever-varying creative energies works its wonders. They fall into two deplorable categories. Some do no thinking whatsoever on this subject, while the rest think they know how to set the standard for everyone. Think of the political blunders based on: "Were all modeled after me, what a wonderful world this would be!" Wrote J. A. Froude in 1860: "Men are made by nature unequal. It is vain, therefore, to treat them as if they were equal."

Assuredly, Froude would agree that every one of us should have equal opportunity to progress creatively as we please and, also, that we should be treated equally by the blindfolded Goddess of Justice. However, he was right in asserting that we are *made* unequal—each of us differing fantastically from any other.

Those who do little if any thinking for themselves are inclined to follow the millions of bunglers who loudly proclaim their know-it-all-ness and promise a heaven on earth. Thus, they fail to heed the very few who speak or

Political Bungling

write the freedom thesis. It is the shouting that leads them astray, drowning out the whispers which might start them on the road to truth.

How do our political bunglers resemble the fictitious firemen previously mentioned? First and foremost, they have no more understanding of how freedom works its wonders than did Cro-Magnon man. Thus blinded to reality, they see what to them appears as a societal flaw, and then employ coercion to correct it. Their remedy does not work. They then double their coercions. Worse than ever: more flaws appear! Deeper into the mire of our present mess! Their cure? More and more of their foolish interventions!

The wiser among us are aware of how little we know; the foolish bunglers are unaware. Wrote the French satirist, Sebastian Chamfort (1741-94): "There are more fools than wise men; and even in wise men, more folly than wisdom."

There is no way accurately to trace these political depravities from their beginnings to present-day socialism. There are literally millions of examples of an initial flaw being "corrected" by an even more serious mistake. Error compounded, and all because of an abysmal know-it-all-ness. Perhaps the following will suffice to make the point.

The bunglers observe that some live in mansions, others in hovels. In 1913 they passed the progressive income tax as an equalizing measure. Senator Borah remarked, "Why, this might go as high as 10%." It went to 91%, perhaps curbing the demand for mansions, but assuredly aggravating the plight of the least affluent who look to the market for supplies.

Their "cures" became progressively worse: minimum wage laws, child labor laws, maximum hours, coercive power granted to labor unions, Medicare, socialized medicine, fraudulent social security, bailing out bankrupt businesses, even to how many dogs one may own and so on. Summarized, these past 66 years have witnessed an increasing application of the Marxian doctrine, "From each according to his ability, to each according to his need."[1]

As I reflect on our political bunglers, I am reminded of a wise observation by Charles Mackay in his remarkable book, *Extraordinary Popular Delusions and the Madness of Crowds,*[2] written in 1841: "Men, it has been well said, think in herds; it will be seen that they go mad in herds, while they only recover their senses slowly and one by one." All human experience, from Cro-Magnon man to the present, attests to this truth. Every good movement in history —no exception—has been led by a handful of men and women who have been fortunate enough to recover their senses.

The socialistic mess we are in is a consequence of the gap between what we are and what we *could* be. The cause of this gap? Our failure to wonder about the unknown potentialities which lie deep in every human soul, and which become apparent only after serious self-examination. The remarkable psychologist, Dr. Fritz Kunkel, revealed a truth which if recognized and pondered day-in-and-day-out would not only expand your and my consciousness but might, now and then, free a politician from his bungling: "*Immense*

---

[1] For an assessment of the extent to which we in the U.S.A. have adopted the ten points of "The Communist Manifesto," see Chapter 15 in my book, *Vision* (Irvington, N.Y.: The Foundation for Economic Education, Inc., 1978).

[2] New York: The Noonday Press, 1969.

hidden powers lurk in the unconscious of the most uncommon man—indeed, of all people without exception."

True, "men are strangely inclined to worship what they do not understand," and the political bunglers are foremost among those so inclined. Well, what's the remedy? Washington Irving (1783-1859) gave good counsel to all of us: "The dullest observer must be sensible of the order and serenity prevalent in those households where the occasional exercise of a beautiful form of worship in the morning gives, as it were, the keynote to every temper for the day, and attunes every spirit to harmony."

The keynote to the good life is freedom. Let every moment be attuned to this blessing!

3
TWO WAYS TO GO WRONG

> *There is a natural and necessary progression from the extreme of anarchy to the extreme of tyranny, and arbitrary power is most easily established on the ruins of liberty.*
> **—GEORGE WASHINGTON**

There are as many ways to go wrong as there are human beings—multiplied by the countless frailties of each individual. This commentary, however, has to do only with two societal evils: anarchy and tyranny—two opposites with much in common.

Anarchy is the absence of any formal agency of society for dealing with aggression, and tyranny in its most vicious form is political control of everyone's actions—socialism in its most pronounced state, as in Russia. Social *dis*organization either way! As Dr. Ludwig von Mises wrote, "Socialism is planned chaos. Anarchy is unplanned chaos."

The Father of our Country was graced with hindsight and foresight. He was aware of the tyranny that had predominated—with a few notable exceptions—throughout recorded history. And he, as much as any American past or present, foresaw and understood the blessings of liberty.

Liberty permits human ascendancy; anarchy and/or tyranny leaves everyone grounded. To pare over-extended government down to its *proper role* is to maximize liberty; it does not represent a halfway house to anarchy. When someone is eating too much of the wrong kind of food, the remedy is not to stop all feeding. This is starvation! The remedy is proper food, in the proper amount.

With the above thoughts in mind, we should never think of liberty—private ownership, free market, limited government—as a way of life halfway between anarchy and tyranny. Rather, we should visualize liberty as a heavenly power releasing human creativity, whereas anarchy/tyranny are restraints of man's potentialities.

Wrote George Santayana: "Tyrants are seldom free; the cares and the instruments of their tyranny *enslave them*." This is just as true of anarchists. Those who believe in no societal agency are also enslaved. In what manner? True, they believe in "protection," but they envision persons or groups hiring their own protectors as they would hire any other type of service. In this degraded way of life each would have his or her own armed guards; the AFL-CIO its own army, the U.S. Chamber of Commerce theirs, and so on. This would result in a society founded, not on enlightened self-interest, but on utter selfishness. Justice impossible!

Wrote Joseph Addison: "Justice disregards party, friendship and kindred, and is therefore represented as blind."

Dr. Benjamin Rogge gave us an accurate assessment as to

how justice is denied by anarchy and tyranny. "The blindfolded Goddess of Justice has been encouraged to peek and she now says, with the jurists of the ancient regime, 'First tell me who you are and then I'll tell you what your rights are.' " A society in which gross inequalities before the law are tolerated will prevent the market from operating in its economic life. Individual liberty depends on the general observance of the principle of equality before the law.

My purpose is not to dwell on the aforementioned ways to go wrong but rather on the *one way* to go right: liberty, that heavenly power which releases human creativity. But, first, a bit of background on some ancient wisdom which links "right" and "left" with "wise" and "foolish." Wrote Confucius 25 centuries ago: "For one word a man is often deemed wise; for one word he is often deemed foolish. We should be careful, indeed, in what we say."

Three centuries later there appeared in Ecclesiastes 10:2 these words. "A wise man's heart inclines him toward the right; but a fool's heart toward the left." What might have been the precise meaning of this when written? Perhaps no one knows. A guess: perhaps today's use of "right" and "left" is a take-off of this ancient axiom.

What a reversal in meaning words have had throughout the ages! As an example, let me quote from Dean Russell's essay entitled *The First Leftist,* written in 1951 when he was a member of FEE's staff:

> The first leftists were a group of newly elected representatives to the National Constituent Assembly at the beginning of the French Revolution in 1789. They were labeled "Leftists" merely because they happened to sit on the left side in the French Assembly.

Two Ways to Go Wrong

The legislators who sat on the right side were referred to as the Party of the Right, or Rightists. The Rightists or "reactionaries" stood for a highly centralized national government, special laws and privileges for unions and various other groups and classes, government economic monopolies in various necessities of life, and government controls over prices, production and distribution.

The ideals of the Party of the Left were based largely on the spirit and principles of our own American Constitution. Those first French Leftists stood for individual freedom of choice and personal responsibility for one's own welfare. Their goal was a peaceful and legal limitation of the powers of the central government, a restoration of local self-government, an independent judiciary, and the abolition of special privileges.

But before the program of those first Leftists was completed, a violent minority *from their own ranks*—the revolutionary Jacobins—grasped the power of government and began their reign of terror and tyranny.

To use a bit of slang, what a switcheroo—"a surprising variation; reversal"—not only in words but in aspirations, ranging from liberty to the ruins of liberty.

Finally, what is the *one* way to go right? What are the ideas that must be understood and adhered to if liberty is to grace our lives? First and foremost is the idea of our dual nature: man is at once an individual and a social being.

It is the purpose of life that each individual, during his or her mortal moments, should approximate Infinite Consciousness as nearly as possible. Righteousness must be our guideline—no deviations, none whatsoever! A good society is impossible unless it is leavened by a few moral exemplars—inspired enough to compose a leadership to which others are attracted. Standard bearers par excellence!

To what extent are we social beings? Almost beyond one's power to imagine! In a highly advanced society—the U.S.A. being more so than any nation past or present—all of us are specialized, and have become *interdependent* as a result. Were we not able to exchange any of our millions of specializations we would perish. Imagine trying to live on what you now do or know how to do?

Free exchange in goods and services and ideas has obstacles galore: power mongers in all walks of life, seekers of countless special privileges and something for nothing—embargoes, tariffs, minimum wages, maximum hours, the Gateway Arch, Medicare—you name it!

The enjoyment of true liberty—everyone free to act creatively—comes not for free but at a very high intellectual, moral and spiritual price: the surmounting—overcoming—of these obstacles. Let us now probe our role as social beings.

If a common justice is to prevail, it is absolutely necessary that there be an agency of society—all of us—to cope with man's inhumanity to man. Liberty and justice are inseparably associated. Wrote Edmund Burke: "Whenever a separation is made between liberty and justice, neither, in my opinion, is safe."

What is the nature of an ideal government? It is where no one "rules" another! Government is an agency of defense, the members of which are you or I or others as social beings. We cast our votes for those who will represent us in keeping the peace and invoking a common justice. Period!

Does the ideal agency use force? Only defensive, never coercive, force. To simplify the distinction, let a policeman

Two Ways to Go Wrong

with a gun stand before your home warding off thieves and other marauders. *Defensive force!* Now—no imagination is necessary for it is all too common—let the policeman enter your home, take your possessions, keep them himself or give to others to obtain their votes. *Coercive force!*

How draw the line between what government should and should not do? This is impossible unless one knows what government is and is not. Government is organized force, issuing edicts and backed by a constabulary, a physical force. This can be symbolized by the clenched fist. Find out what the fist can and cannot do and we will know what government *should* and *should not* do.

This physical force can repel and restrain, in a word, inhibit. What, in all good conscience, *should* be inhibited? The moral codes give the answer: fraud, violence, misrepresentation—thou shalt not steal or kill or do any evil. And government cannot perform this role when overstepping its proper bounds. For proof, merely observe the extent to which coercive force has replaced defensive force.

In what realm is this physical force absolutely impotent, majority opinion to the contrary notwithstanding? In the realm of the creative! All the goods and services by which we live and prosper show forth in the spiritual before they manifest themselves in the material, that is, in the sense that discoveries, inventions, insights, intuitive flashes are spiritual. There would be no such thing as an ordinary glass had not some cave dweller eons ago *discovered* how to harness fire. Airplanes? Out of the question had not a Hindu *invented* the concept of zero. All modern chemistry, physics and so on would be no more than dreams had we to rely on Roman numerals.

So, how shall we draw the line? Limit government to inhibiting the wrong, and leave all creative actions—education or whatever—to men acting freely, competitively, privately, cooperatively, voluntarily!

As George Washington asserted: " . . . arbitrary power [socialism] is most easily established on the ruins of liberty." Likewise, the power to act creatively as we please can be easily established on the ruins of socialism. The *one right way* is simple: grasp the error of socialism and the truth of liberty. As noted in John 8:32: *The truth shall make you free.*

4
THE PRETENDER'S PLAGUE

There is a false modesty, which is vanity; a false glory, which is levity; a false grandeur, which is uneasiness; a false virtue, which is hypocrisy, and a false wisdom which is prudery.
—JEAN DE LA BRUYÈRE

Humanity has suffered all sorts of plagues, and some of them have changed the course of history. The Black Death of the 14th century reduced the population of Europe and Asia by three fourths and had enormous social consequences. Then there are plagues of a different sort, such as the plague of present-day "pretenders." Medical science has rid the world of the former and only some remarkable thinking can do away with the latter. Succeed, or we face another population disaster. Jean de La Bruyère (1645-96), French essayist and moralist, gave us some excellent guidelines. Let us reflect on their meaning.

There is a false modesty, which is vanity. Modesty is defined as "unassuming or humble behavior; lack of excesses or *pretension;* decency; decorum." Interesting are the varying and contradictory assessments of modesty. Here are two among ever so many examples by famous thinkers:

> The first of all virtues is innocence, the next is modesty.
> —*Joseph Addison* (1672-1719)

> Modesty is the lowest of all virtues and is a confession of the deficiency it indicates. He who undervalues himself, is justly undervalued by others.
> —*William Hazlitt* (1778-1830)

And here is one that squares with La Bruyère's point:

> A *false* modesty is the meanest species of pride.
> —*Edward Gibbon* (1737-94)

If we accept the dictionary's definition—and I do—then those who are modest are definitely not pretenders. And modesty is a virtue second to innocence only when the individual acknowledges his innocence relative to the Infinite. In other words, he is aware of how little he knows. No false modesty here!

A false modesty is, indeed, vanity—"the quality of being excessively proud of oneself." Wrote the English poet, John Gay, "Pride is increased by ignorance; *those assume the most who know the least.*" A large percentage of our elected and appointed officials are afflicted with this false modesty—they know so little, yet they "know" how to run our lives! Obsessed with the power of office, they allow their own lives to run out of control. Assuredly, this is the origin of vanity!

A false glory which is levity. What is levity? Says the dictionary: "... improper or unbecoming gaiety or flippancy; lack of seriousness; fickleness, instability." False glory, in short, is outward show concealing inner emptiness. William Cowper (1731-1800), bequeathed posterity a good definition of false glory: "Glory, built on selfish principles is shame and guilt."

Goethe added his wisdom: "By skillful conduct and artificial means a person may make a sort of name for himself; but if the *inner jewel* be wanting, all is vanity, and will not last."

The inner jewel? The Scottish judge, Henry Home (1696-1782) had an excellent answer: "The shortest way to glory is to be guided by conscience."

Reflect on the vast majority of citizens, in and out of office, whose lives are built on selfish principles which feather their own nests at the expense of others. These "principles" range all the way from food stamps to rent control to free lunches to social security to medicare to government swimming pools. There are thousands of these!

One point we must keep in mind: the distinction between selfishness and self-interest. Selfish? It is "having such regard for one's own interests and advantage that the happiness and welfare of others become of less concern than is considered right or just."

As to self-interest, no one, to my knowledge, ever gave a better explanation than William Graham Sumner: "Making the most of one's self . . . is not a separate thing from filling one's place in society, but *the two are one,* and the latter is accomplished when the former is done."

A false grandeur, which is uneasiness. Grandeur is "greatness of position, eminence . . . a moral and intellectual greatness." Obviously, a false grandeur is the opposite, namely, an overestimation of self—unbridled pride.

In Ezekiel 21:26 we find: "The Holy One (blessed be He) raises those who humble themselves, and *degrades those who are of a proud spirit.*" Uneasiness is the want of ease or tranquility or peacefulness. It is, indeed, the penalty of pride.

A false virtue, which is hypocrisy. Virtue is "general moral excellence; right action and thinking." In my judgment, virtue is attainable to the extent that a person *strictly* adheres to whatever his or her highest consciousness dictates as righteous.

What, then, is false virtue? It is a refusal to be guided by the highest moral principles—the Ten Commandments and The Golden Rule—and a yielding instead to such unholy attractions as popularity, fame, power over others and the like. This is vice—". . . moral failing; corruption, depravity." And vice nearly always pretends to be what it is not. Hypocrisy!

Hypocrites are pretenders—the plague of mankind.

A false wisdom which is prudery. This observation conveys the same implications as the previous one, for is not false wisdom a false virtue? And prudery—"exaggerated modesty in behavior"—certainly borders on hypocrisy.

Why does this author express the same thought in different words? Words have varied meanings from time to time, and thus strike listeners and readers differently at different periods. Finding words for common sense is an exploration that has no ending.

Take the word "meek" for example. Originally, it was

inwethan, in the Aramaic. When translated to Greek, the word became *praos*. The French translated it as *debonair*. In English at the time of the King James version of the Bible, and even before, the word "meek" implied "a wonderful, inherent, teachability." The Beatitude means, therefore, that "the teachable shall inherit the earth." In our time "meek" implies "timid, shrinking, apologetic."

Wrote Tryon Edwards: "Words are both better and worse than thoughts; they express them, and add to them; they give them power for good or evil; they start them on an endless flight, for instruction and comfort and blessing, or for injury and sorrow and ruin." Let us find words for instruction, comfort and blessing, never for injury, sorrow and ruin.

Nature never pretends. May we follow her example!

5

POLITICAL STEALING

If from my thousand pecks you steal but one my loss is small, but you're by sin undone. **—HORACE**

Nearly all adult Americans think they know what stealing is; it is the seizure of another's property by force or fraud. Were there no more to stealing than outright thievery—including its causes and consequences—we would leave the problem to our local policemen, assuming their defensive competency.

Political stealing, however, is so common, on such an enormous scale, and practiced or advocated by citizens in all walks of life—teachers, preachers, businessmen, politicians, and so on—that it is far more approved than condemned. It has become our way of life—and death—and may indeed be our greatest problem. So let us begin our homework!

Horace, the Roman poet of 2000 years ago, was not referring to political theft, but to stealing by individual thieves. His statement, as related to our times, might read, "If from my thousand possessions someone steals but one—a watch, for instance—my loss is small but his sin will do him in." The apprehended thief is undone, indeed! No

Political Stealing

one will hire or trust or trade with him. A societal dropout—a lost soul!

There is no way of knowing how many of these lost souls plague our lives. Assuredly, they constitute but a fraction of the population. During my 81 years, I have been robbed twice—$10 by a pickpocket and later $150 by another of that despicable ilk—surely not an unbearable drain upon my time or possessions.

What accounts for such thievery? There are reasons galore, most of which are unknown even to these bandits. There is one generality: an absence of moral scruples. They have no aim in life beyond something for nothing. Thus, they commit their sins unknowingly. Ignorance in the driver's seat!

Political stealing is mass degradation. It is a collusion between our 16,000,000 elected and appointed office holders and most of our 180,000,000 adult citizens. Most of those in both categories commit their crimes unknowingly, as do the individual thieves. Interestingly, the motivation is the same: something for nothing!

A wise observation: "He sins as much who holds the sack as he who fills it." This is to say that the recipients of loot are as sinful as are the political looters. Right!

Who are the sack holders? They range from paupers to millionaires. In most cases, the wealthy individuals, along with nearly everyone else, accept Medicare when reaching the age of 65. Medicare provides a government subsidy in the event of illness. The source of this illicit loot? Everyone who pays taxes, including the paupers! How explain? Medicare, like thousands of other government "enterprises"—social security, the Gateway Arch, TVA, urban renewal and the like—is "financed" by inflating the money supply to drain goods and services from the market, thus increasing the cost of remaining supplies. Result? The poor become poorer!

This vicious trend is often described as a contest between the "haves" and the "have nots"—the taking of livelihood from the wealthy and passing it on to the poor—as if this were only a dollar and cents problem. Assessing the matter realistically, the "have nots" include those in all walks of life. A few of many examples:

- The poor *have not* an opening for jobs by reason of minimum wage laws.
- Ever so many workers *have not* the opportunity to free themselves from labor-union dictation.
- Businessmen *have not* the right to free exchange by reason of trade restrictions.
- Youth *have not* the right to work: child labor laws.
- Many teachers *have not* the privilege of explaining the virtues of freedom: government education.

If the poor, the so-called beneficiaries, were to realize that they are being robbed rather than helped, there would be a quick end to this politico-economic insanity. Your and my role? To see how much enlightenment we can gain and share.

There may be no better way to get at the root of this problem than to cite and explain the Eighth Commandment: *Thou shalt not steal*. Our troubles stem, as previously asserted, from an absence of moral scruples. This Commandment ranks high among all the moral injunctions. Why?

Stealing is wrong because owning is good. *Stealing pre-*

supposes ownership! TVA will serve to make the point. My earnings were and are coercively expropriated by taxation to subsidize TVA's construction and year-to-year losses, but I have *no control* over its performance. Something I owned—a part of my earnings—was taken to build TVA, but I *own* no part of it—not a penny's worth! The government "owns" TVA.

How are we to draw the distinction between political and private ownership? There may be no better answer than *self-responsibility*. In ventures based on government "ownership," not a single political official feels that failure is his responsibility. The loss falls in the lap of no one in particular. Thus, no one does his best.

In the use of privately owned property, the outcome is in the individual's lap. I am responsible for mine and you for yours. Self-interest inspires the best that is within each of us. The Biblical injunction, "Thou shalt not steal," could have no other reference than to private ownership. How can one steal that which is not privately owned? Absurd!

The freedom way of life can be defined thus: *Private ownership,* free market, limited government with its moral and spiritual antecedents. Private ownership is the foundation of freedom. Omit this and there can be no free market. The despicable alternative is government "ownership" which has no moral and spiritual antecedents.

Wrote Tryon Edwards: "Sin with the multitude, and your responsibility and guilt are as great and as truly personal as if *you alone* had done the wrong."

The alternative? Instead of sinning, pursue righteousness. Side with Henry Clay: *"I would rather be right than be President!"*

6

LIVING: BY ROTE OR BY WHAT'S RIGHT

> *We first make our habits, and then habits make us.*
> *All habits gather, by unseen degrees, as brooks make rivers, rivers run to seas.*
> **—JOHN DRYDEN**

Rote is defined thus: "by memory alone, without understanding or thought." Doubtless, this is why the English poet and author, John Dryden (1631-1700), used the word "habit," for its definition is: ". . . a settled tendency of behavior or normal . . . manner or procedure; a custom or practice, as a habit of rivers."

There are, of course, excellent habits that are indispensable to doing what's right. More later on that point. The initial reference will be to "habit" as synonymous with "rote"—repetitious behaviors that lack understanding and thought.

Probably no one above the moronic level lives by rote in

Living: By Rote or By What's Right

all aspects of life. Were this the case, civilization would be at an end. However, the extent to which this intellectual deathtrap prevails determines how sluggish—lacking in vigor—will be our advancement.

Prayer by rote is common to millions of church members, despite Jesus' admonition: "Use not vain repetitions, as the heathen do." They merely repeat the words of some original thinker without any thought of their own. Are such vacuous prayers ever heard? Doubtful!

Time after time I have been in small and large luncheon and dinner groups where they all stand, bow their heads, place their right hands over their hearts and pledge allegiance to our flag. With few exceptions, this is but a formality, patriotism only in spelling—oblivious to what the American flag symbolizes.

For a gigantic example of living by rote, have a look at our present-day politico-economic behavior. It borders on the indescribable. How account for this depravity? Jacques Barzun gave a valid answer: "Intellect deteriorates after every surrender to folly. Unless we *consciously* resist, the nonsense does not pass us by but into us."[1]

Approximately one-ninth of our adult population are elected or appointed government officials—16,000,000 federal, state and local! It is impossible to estimate the nonsense they engender. Fortunately, not a single person hears or reads anywhere near one per cent of it! But, without question, more than 99 per cent of the population unwittingly absorbs and responds to this political verbiage, and while rarely heeding the words of our few statesmen.

---

[1] See *The House of Intellect* (New York: Harper & Bros., 1959), p. 222.

Why this surrender to folly? Why does intellect deteriorate? It is because of an all-too-common inability *consciously* to resist. As a consequence, the nonsense, instead of passing by, goes into—becomes a part of—most citizens. Anyway, this is enough of a commentary on those who, in many aspects of this mortal life, live by rote!

It is now appropriate to reflect on those excellent habits which are indispensable to doing what's right. John Tillotson, Archbishop of Canterbury (1630-94) had an enlightening thought: "When we have practised good actions awhile, they become easy; when they are easy, we take pleasure in them; when they please us, we do them frequently; and then, by frequency of act, they grow into a habit."

When we have practised good actions awhile, they became easy. Good actions are impossible without practice. Take any activity, be it golf or cooking or writing or speaking or whatever, the more practice the easier.

When we were in first grade learning to write we had to think our way around each letter of the alphabet. Today as adults? Those physical movements have been relegated to the conditioned reflexes and all we have to think about is what we wish to say.

The lesson to be derived from this? Advance to that level of understanding where we can explain the fallacies of socialism and the righteousness of freedom with the same ease as we can give the answer to "What's 6 times 7?"

Most of us derive pleasure from countless blessings: good health, good friends, a plenitude of goods and services, vacations, occupational success, and so on. Nothing wrong with most of these.

Then there are those who get pleasure from political

power, notoriety, running the lives of others and similar forms of nonsense. Reflecting on this kind of "pleasure," the American clergyman, Richard Fuller (1808-76) wrote: "Worldly and sensual pleasures, for the most part, are short, false and deceitful! Like drunkenness, they revenge the jolly madness of one hour with the sad repentance of many."

Archbishop Tillotson had a superior goal in mind. Pleasure—enjoyment of the higher order—is possible only as we live a life of virtue and justice: righteousness!

When they are easy, we take pleasure in them. There are tiny phases of the freedom philosophy that some individuals find easy. And pleasurable, indeed, are these accomplishments!

Wrote Herbert Spencer: " 'Easy come, easy go,' is as applicable to knowledge as to wealth." All of us are acquainted with individuals who by a streak of luck become wealthy. Luck, however, is not the result of effort nor proportioned to merit, that is, it has no foundation—easy come, easy go!

Those who find phases of the freedom way of life easy to explain have made righteousness their first aim in life—all else secondary. All gains are gratifying and enjoyable!

When they please us, we do them frequently. A single step in the right philosophical direction—toward freedom—does far more than please the doers thereof. Like a magnetic force, the success of the first step beckons that person and others to take additional steps. And this power of attraction doubles and quadruples—on and on—frequency unlimited!

By frequency of act, they grow into a habit. When our primary mode of action is the private ownership, free market, limited government way of life with its moral and spiritual antecedents, the right will, indeed, become not only frequent but perpetual. And if that is not habit-forming, pray tell, what is!

Let me conclude with an unusual thought inspired by the preceding paragraphs. Should those of us who live by what's right—and not rote—*advocate* the right of everyone to act creatively as he or she pleases? No, for the spirit of advocacy does not jibe with Divine Sources. No one advocates that the earth become a spheroid! Neither freedom nor the shape of our planet is a subject for advocacy; both are *facts for affirmation!*

Affirm the Divine in word and deed!

7

AUTHORITY: TO BE EMBRACED OR REJECTED?

*Authority intoxicates,
And makes sots of magistrates;
The fumes of it invade the brain,
And make men giddy, proud, and
vain.* **—SAMUEL BUTLER**

There are two opposed types of authority. There is, first, the kind of authority conveyed by the unvarnished truth to receptive minds; the second is symbolized by the club—naked force. The former gains the assent of the will; it is voluntary cooperation. The latter overrides the will; it is antagonistic and coercive. I like the old theological vocabulary which would label the one, heavenly, the other, hellish; it is the contrast between (a) the Source of Truth, and (b) the forcible imposition of nonsense.

There is only one Source of Truth: Infinite Consciousness—Creation. There are, however, many subsidiary sources, namely, those seers, past and present, who have surpassed the mill run of us in their ability to intercept the wisdom of Divine Omnipotence. Whenever we seek enlightenment, we can learn from them just as they have learned from The Source. Indeed, if we fully realize our potentialities, we may become helpful subsidiaries ourselves, and the source of light to other seekers.

The above aspirations would be extremely difficult to achieve, if not impossible, without a minimal coercive authority. I refer to a government *strictly* limited to inhibiting all destructive human actions, leaving everyone free to act creatively as each chooses. Our freedom depends upon such a defensive force against the coercive acts of others.

The above are authorities we should embrace. Now to the object of this thesis—the authorities we should reject.

The English statesman, Lord Acton (1834-1902), a distinguished liberal in the classical sense and a devout Roman Catholic, wrote, "Power tends to corrupt and absolute power corrupts absolutely." This shocking truth was inspired by the *infallibility* assumed by some of those in the papal hierarchy. It is obvious that no human remotely approaches infallibility. Lord Acton had the courage to pronounce the results: absolutely corrupting to the practitioners thereof. It leads to the forcible imposition of nonsense!

The English poet, Samuel Butler (1612-80), two centuries prior to Lord Acton, saw through the sham of power mongers—authority over the life of others—and beautifully phrased the end results: "Makes sots of magistrates." A sot? "Stupid like a habitual drunkard."

True, no more than a few among the millions of sots would fall into this intellectual gutter were they aware of (1) how it destroys their own lives and (2) the disaster it inflicts

Authority: To Be Embraced or Rejected?

on all citizens. Why this inebriation? The answer may lie much deeper than we think. Here is one that deserves reflection.

Bear in mind that whatever shows forth on the political horizon is but an echoing or reflection of the given society's preponderant leadership thinking at the time. If this assessment be correct, then it is today's "thinking" that accounts for the countless sots who presently bedevil our country—those "infallibles" who would cast us in their little warped images. What lies at the root of their "thinking"?

It is inherent in the very nature of man to be led from the what-is toward the what-ought-to-be. Evolution is implicit in the Cosmic Scheme, and mankind today is far more evolved than Cro-Magnon man. The Creation which created us is a magnetic force. It is *the* first and foremost Law of Attraction.

Who can or cannot be drawn toward this Cosmic Order? Only the receptive. To symbolize the answer, take a handful of particles composed mostly of sawdust and a few iron or steel filings. Place a magnet over the particles and observe that only the filings are drawn to it.

Millions of people in the modern world—symbolized by the sawdust—are not attracted to the Cosmic Magnet. Some of these live aimless lives, but many others are powerfully drawn to the political messiahs who lead the collectivist movements of our time—Marxists and their ilk. A kind of mass hysteria results, and the silly seeds are sown which take root and sprout into "sottish magistrates."

Wrote Plato: "The punishment of wise men who refuse to take part in the affairs of government *is to live under the government of unwise men.*"

How shall we define "wise men"? My answer: *The more they know, the greater is their awareness of how little they know.* Those who grasp this Socratic wisdom concentrate on self-improvement; there is not an iota of be-like-me-ness in their make-up. They would no more think of telling a neighbor how to run his or her life than dictating how Creation should be modified. Intellectually, morally and spiritually, they are the very opposite of the unwise ones who aspire to dictatorial powers. This is another way of saying that they are the opposite of Marxists—socialists. As a consequence, they are free-market oriented, believing that all citizens should be free to act creatively as they please.

Presently, with some notable exceptions, we are living under government by unwise men. And the reason is that many of the wise men among us, lacking political aspirations themselves, mistakenly assume that what government does is none of their business. They fail to see what they could and should be doing to limit government to its principled role of keeping the peace with justice to all.

Even the wisest are imperfect. Many have unwisely overlooked the method they should employ: getting so proficient at understanding and explaining the freedom philosophy that others will look to them as mentors. Our wise men have attained their present heights by intercepting Creation's Law of Attraction. It follows that they should apply this Divine Principle at the human level. It has worked for them and it can have a comparable effect on others.

To repeat, what shows forth on the political horizon is but a reflection of the preponderant thinking, be it unwise or wise. What, then, is the role of wise men? *It is neither silence nor reforming the unwise!* Wrote Henri Frederic

Authority: To Be Embraced or Rejected?   39

Amiel (1821-81): "Truth is not only violated by falsehood; it may be equally outraged by silence." We are further enlightened by Michel E. de Montaigne (1533-92): "Reform only yourself; for in doing that you do everything."

The formula is simple: Let each freedom devotee become so proficient that others will single out these wise men as mentors!

Instead of silence, there will be oral and written explanations sharing with all who seek. The more one shares, the more will he or she be graced with higher grade thoughts. This growth, and it alone, energizes the magnetism that draws others. It is the Law of Attraction at the human level!

And now for the good tidings. Among the seekers will be wise men replacing "sottish magistrates" in governmental offices, statesmen replacing politicians, that is, those who seek truth and not power over a single creative action! Several of the benefits we can expect:

1—A limited government staffed by statesmen numbering but a tiny fraction of the present political multitude.
2—Inflation will be at an end.
3—No more strikes or tariffs or any other restrictions to creative actions.
4—Free traders, the only ambassadors of good will, replacing politicians as the U.S.A.'s representatives in other nations.
5—All Americans as free to exchange goods and services with those in other countries as with those in our fifty states.
6—A rebirth of the American Miracle and socialism a bygone nightmare!

Let us reject authoritarians and all of their intoxications

and corruptions and, instead, heed and abide by the counsel of George Washington: "If, to please the people, we offer what we ourselves disapprove, how can we afterwards defend our work? Let us raise a standard to which *the wise and honest* can repair. The event is in the hand of God."

8

GOOD DOERS OR DO-GOODERS?

Fenelon learned that his library was on fire: "God be praised," he said, "that it is not the dwelling of some poor man."
—WILLIAM DEAN HOWELLS

Howells (1837-1920), American author, by quoting the above, demonstrated an unusual trait, namely, the ability to recognize a *good doer,* a benevolent individual, on reading his thoughts. Howells may or may not have had an awareness of the opposite type, a malevolent individual—a do-gooder.

François Fenelon (1651-1715), French theologian, author, Archbishop of Cambria and a great scholar, assuredly had a large and valuable library. Yet with rare and benevolent attitude, he could accept its loss in full compassion for others less fortunate. A *good doer,* par excellence.

In contrast are the countless do-gooders. According to my

dictionary, they are "impractical minded humanitarians bent on promoting welfare work or reform." Let me modify the thoughts of another:

> Avoid an angry man for a while, a malevolent one forever.
>
> The violence and evil of our time have been, when viewed collectively, the work, of impotent men who seek power in order to conceal their failure as persons. They are repressed and frustrated, taking refuge in a system of "thought" or a mode of life into which doing good cannot intrude. These bewildered individuals from Hitler downward advocate violence as a means of inflicting their nefarious ways on all of us. Result? Societal disintegration!

The late Newton Dillaway, a brilliant gentleman and outstanding biographer of Ralph Waldo Emerson, wrote numerous exposures of our "bewildered individuals." He asks this fundamental question: "Is God to be pigeon-holed by the whims of man?" Several of his answers:

> A system of fixed concepts is contrary to the natural law. It prevents life from flowing. It prevents the passage of the Universal Law.
>
> More damage is done than we realize in trying to force human situations—whether in diet or metaphysics, whether in training children or in planning the social order.
>
> Life asks only that we flow *with it,* that we do not resist, that we do not crawl into corners and erect barriers.[1]

---

[1] See *Consent* by Newton Dillaway (Unity Books, Unity Village, Missouri).

Good Doers or Do-Gooders?

Another name for "do-gooders" is "mean-wellers." These people are unaware that everything we know is an interception of the Universal Law, and so they are addicted to fixed concepts—their fixings, *coercively implemented!* They are well intentioned, but so was Cro-Magnon man of 35,000 years ago and, earlier still, the cave dwellers. These "mean-wellers" hinder life from flowing because they are innocently ignorant of any such phenomenal process.

More damage is done than we realize in trying to force human behavior. Suppose Emerson, Dillaway's intellectual, moral and spiritual hero, had used force to cast others in his image—"Behave as I say or I shall force you to do so." What would be the result were *everyone* so directed and restricted? Emerson's brilliant writings would have come to an end! Why? He would have starved to death! Imagine living on only what he did or the output of your specialized efforts! Or, suppose one's energies were devoted *exclusively* to making the case for freedom. Live on that and nothing else? Perish the absurd thought!

Let's try to dramatize this quandary. A famous painter—Pablo Picasso—favored political dictatorship—the state his god. Would you seek his explanation as to how the free market works its wonders?

Frederic Bastiat, on the other hand, was one of the greatest contributors of all time to how the free market works its wonders. But, would you ask him to paint a portrait of the Scottish economist, Adam Smith? Might as well ask me how to make a pencil!

To aid in understanding the destructive actions of "do-gooders" and "mean-wellers," why not add the word *smother* to the ones commonly used: stifle, squelch, inhibit, restrain? These millions smother—take the living breath out of—creativity. Were our population composed only of these little dictocrats, there would be no pencils, no food, no life.

Wrote William Wordsworth (1770-1850): "Life is divided into three terms—that which was, which is, and which shall be. Let us *learn* from the past to profit by the present, and from the present to live better for the future."

If anyone wonders what Dillaway meant by "Life asks only that we flow with it," our English poet, quoted above, gave the answer nearly two centuries earlier. And what a splendid formula for individual emergence—life's high purpose!

That which was. Most present-day Americans have all but forgotten the foundations of our country—the Declaration, Constitution and Bill of Rights. True, many pay obeisance to these documents as a formality but, unfortunately, are unaware of their essence. Which was? Government more limited than ever before in all history. The fruits of this wisdom? Self-reliance, self-responsibility, freedom of choice, freedom to compete and to produce and exchange goods and services, culminating in *The American Miracle!* The right answer to life: all talents freely flowing! General prosperity as a result!

That which is. Except for the very few who are intellectually alert and keenly aware of the *what was,* the prosperity we all enjoy has wreaked its damage on our population. Politico-economic talents lie dormant. The merit of government limited to keeping the peace and invoking a common justice is no more apprehended by our contemporaries than it was by England's mercantilists!

How account for the present dormancy? The unprecedented affluence which graces the lives of the multitudes is disproportionate to the efforts, on their part, to achieve it. As a consequence, they fail to think of affluence as a gift of a free economy.

Only a people who struggle for what they obtain will highly prize it. What is theirs will be lightly parted with if it is acquired without effort. Being born with a silver spoon or into a highly efficient economy may be a far greater handicap to one's emergence than being born poor. Today, millions of Americans are wealthy who have done nothing toward the acquisition of their wealth. It wouldn't be quite so bad if they only had the insight to understand that affluence is a by-product of freedom.

That which shall be. The do-gooders are still in the driver's seat. Can they be unseated? Yes, if we accept and emulate Abraham Lincoln's counsel: "The occasion is piled high with difficulty, and we must rise high with the occasion."

Rising high with the occasion must include an ever-greater faith that we will win. Emerson suggested the appropriate formula: "All I have seen teaches me to *trust the Creator* for all I have not seen."

We have not seen François Fenelon but we know of his high ideals. Also, we are aware of numerous good-doers.

The do-gooders will lose their power over us when and if you and I *join the good-doers!*

9

FICKLE CONTRADICTIONS

A virtuous tyrant is a contradiction in terms.
—BENJAMIN JOWETT

To contradict someone means, generally, to assert the opposite of what he has spoken or written. Contradictions fall into two categories: some are sincere, thoughtful, honest; but others are merely fickle—by which I mean tricky, deceitful, unstable.

Actually, if one is improving from day to day, present positions differ from or even contradict those believed earlier. And ever so many differences divide those of us devoted to freedom, especially as to methods of advancing it. These sincere differences, however, are not the aim of this brevity.

What then? A commentary on the fickle contradictions which, in today's America, are rapidly on the increase and

Fickle Contradictions

seriously threaten our high aspiration—freedom. These are so many that a mere sampling must suffice. These may help me and some others to distinguish the fickle from the sincere.

Benjamin Jowett (1817-93), was a classical scholar at Oxford, a translator of Plato and Aristotle, and a philosopher in his own right. What a wise and needed observation: A *virtuous tyrant is a contradiction in terms!* In ancient Greece a tyrant was one who seized sovereignty, a usurper. In our time, it includes "any person who exercises his authority in an oppressive manner." We have them by the millions! Virtue? Says the dictionary: "right action and thinking; moral excellence." So, how can tyranny be virtuous?

Interestingly, we never hear anyone use such contradictory expressions as "gentle murderer" or "generous robber" or "wise idiot." Yet, observe the mass approval of those who rob Peter to pay Paul. Virtue is ascribed to those who advocate and practice the Marxian dictum, "from each according to his ability, to each according to his need." Tyranny has acquired the appearance of virtue!

Appearances, however, are often false. Tyranny is not a virtue but the very opposite—*a sin! In a sacred Hindu text–the Bhagavad-Gita* —we read this wisdom: "Sin is not the violation of a law or convention . . . but ignorance . . . which seeks its own private gain at the expense of others."

Living at the expense of others—tyranny—assumes the dimensions of mass hysteria. And it is ignorance which allows such tyranny to be commonly regarded as a virtue, hence the contradiction in terms.

Government education, featured by compulsory attendance, government dictated curricula, and the forcible collection of the wherewithal to pay the bills is, also, a contradiction in terms. True education is achieved by *seeking enlightenment—learning!*

Truth can no more be forced into the mind of another than can humility, love, graciousness or an awareness of human limitations. Those who resort to force—coercion—trying to dictate to others how to think and act, violate the first Commandment: "Thou shalt have no other gods before me." Without knowing it, they presume to be God.[1]

All fickle notions are neither more nor less than ferments of the mind. Reflect on how such simple truths as these—two among thousands—contradict popular "thinking":

1—When and if inflation brings our legal tender near to zero, the dollar will no longer be money.
2—A frozen wage or price is no longer a wage or price; they are mere political numerals backed by force!

This last point brings to mind one of the most fickle contradictions of all: popular belief in *the right to strike*. But, first, how in this lamentable and unforgivable instance should "right" be defined? Let that brilliant German philosopher, Immanuel Kant (1724-1804), give the answer appropriate to his, our and all time: "Act *only* on that maxim [principle] through which you can at the same time *will that it should become a universal law.*"

How shall a strike be defined and when does it really begin? Not when one quits his or her employment! This

---

[1] For a detailed explanation of why education should be left to the free and unfettered market where the wisdom is, see chapters 15, 16 and 17 in my book, *Anything That's Peaceful* (Irvington, N.Y.: The Foundation for Economic Education, Inc., 1964).

right is precious and should be allowed to everyone. Nor is it when workers quit in unison. The strike begins only when workers quit their jobs in unison and *use brute force to keep others from filling the jobs they have vacated!*

Using Kant's maxim, is this a right that should become a universal law? My answer is an unqualified "No!" And so, I think, must be the answer of any reasonable person who fully grasps the consequences of such coercive action.

For instance, let us suppose that the flight attendants or the maintenance crews of an airline have gone on strike. Now imagine this as a universal law—everyone doing it. The airlines, of course, would cease to operate. But now extend the strike to include all growers and suppliers of food, manufacturers, physicians, telephone operators, producers of electricity, and every other contributor to life and livelihood. Chaos! All would perish!

But strikes are not limited to labor unions! Every businessman who advocates restrictions against free production and trade is a striker against the welfare of mankind. Every teacher, preacher, politician or anyone else who proposes restraints against the release of creative human energy is a striker. Some of us may be far less inclined to strike than are others. But in our imperfect human condition, where is the individual who does not and would not try to exercise his striking power?

Surface appearances suggest that the odds are overwhelmingly against the goose that lays the golden eggs—freedom to act creatively. But look beneath the surface and we may see a different picture.

Reflect on the nature of adversity. It can be likened to a physical force having two possible consequences:

1—Adversity can run over and destroy our society.
2—It is possible that adversity resisted may give us the strength to hurdle these "virtuous tyrants."

In every lemon is the potential for lemonade. Likewise, in every adversity is the opportunity to rise above it, providing that these trials and tribulations are regarded as possible sources of strength. Obstacles may become steppingstones.

Shangri-La, for example—a dreamland of milk and honey—has no obstacles; it is hellish in that all humans would lose their strength in Shangri-La. Is it not obvious that we tend to rise only to such heights as our obstacles and adversaries demand? True, some they destroy; but others, the ones fortunate enough to preserve freedom, gain strength from these adverse forces.

Wrote the English critic and author, William Hazlitt (1778-1830): "Prosperity is a great teacher; adversity is a greater. Possession pampers the mind; privation trains and strengthens it." In that sense, let us be grateful to the "virtuous tyrants" who spur us to resist and overcome.

10

"ABOUT FACE": REFORMERS!

Be not angry that you cannot make others as you wish them to be, since you cannot make yourself as you wish to be.
—**THOMAS à KEMPIS**

As a solider overseas in WW I, I often heard and obeyed the command, "About Face." This merely meant to do a turnabout—face and march in the opposite direction. And that's my theme as related to those who would reform their fellowmen.

The thought expressed above by Thomas à Kempis (1380-1471) was in accord with the thinking of another great philosopher 1,000 years earlier, Saint Augustine (354-430 A.D.), Bishop of Hippo. This thinker entitled his autobiography, *Confessions*. Even today, fifteen centuries after his passing, it is still the most widely read autobiography of all time! Among the many bits of wisdom passed on to posterity is this: strive for that excellence in understanding which will cause others to seek one's tutorship. Briefly, resort to the law of attraction.

Examine any one of countless occupational endeavors—golf, cooking, medicine, artistry or whatever—and note that those out front attract emulators. Example: Golfers at my Club do not ask me how to play golf; but wave a magic wand and put Jack Nicklaus in my place and every member will try to learn from him. As I have learned from Charles Kingsley: "Nothing is so infectious as example."

Let me share a favorite verse, author unknown:

> And so I hold it is not treason
> To advance a simple reason
> For the sorry lack of progress we decry.
> It is this: Instead of working
> On himself, each man is shirking
> And trying to reform some other guy.

To reform others would require the transplanting of talents—utterly impossible. There are all kinds of talents—millions of them—not one of which can be transplanted. Personal talents range from gymnastics to deep-sea exploration to writing and speaking on countless subjects to piloting airplanes to composing Grand Opera to an expertise in optometry, cooking, needle point—you name it! Could Leonardo da Vinci have transplanted in me that extraordinary talent of his which produced the famous Mona Lisa? No more than you could transplant into another whatever your unique talent happens to be!

Who are those so vigorously "trying to reform some other guy"? They are all the citizens who bemoan the "sorry lack of progress we decry"—the mess we are in—and who pay no heed to self-improvement. Suppose they were to succeed. Suppose everyone were to become carbon copies of

"About Face": Reformers! 53

them, that is, a world of *reformers*. The result would be unpleasant—a world of *deformers!*

Let us now reflect on a world of *informers,* those from whom others seek information—enlightenment.

Many of the best informers of all time were not college graduates, indeed, some of the greatest never went to school: Confucius, Jesus of Nazareth, Socrates. Abraham Lincoln was little more than a first grader and Andrew Carnegie, the great industrialist, had only three months of schooling. Wisdom may indeed come from humble sources. Look for light in whomever it shines!

Indeed, one of the most striking examples is the wisdom that came from the mind of a Roman slave—Epictetus. This slave became a learned Stoic, embracing the philosophy which holds that all happenings are the result of divine will and that, therefore, man should be free from passion and grief.

Stoicism was so at odds with the "thinking" of Roman Emperor Domitian, who reigned 81-96 A.D., that he exiled many philosophers, including the remarkable slave. Epictetus was sent by sea to the little town of Nicopolis, northeast of Athens.

There he conducted his own school, and was so well regarded and highly esteemed that he established the reputation of the place as Town of Epictetus' School. Students came from Athens and Rome to attend classes. Private citizens came to ask his advice and guidance. Many of his students on returning home assumed the philosophic way of life *in order to escape into the sphere of stoic freedom.*

The wisdom of Epictetus comes to us in large part through *The Enchiridion,* a small book of notes taken by one of his students and translated into numerous languages.[1] Such is the lasting line of transmission and influence of the seeker after truth—the informer. If Epictetus had sought to reform others, force them into his mold, his thoughts would have been buried along with him—a historic zero.

But Epictetus was one of history's outstanding informers, an individual worthy of our emulation. His thoughts, instead of dying on the vine, live on to this day and the end is not in sight. *The Enchiridion* has had enormous influence on great truth seekers, men who lived more than 15 centuries after him: Montaigne, Grotius, Descartes, Montesquieu, Adam Smith, Immanuel Kant and ever so many others.

Until recently, Epictetus was only a name to me: I would have confessed to knowing nothing of his philosophy. Yet, on reflection, I know much of it. For so great has been his influence on those whose writings are familiar to me that I have been, quite unconsciously, the beneficiary of his truth seeking. Here I am, nearly twenty centuries later, looking up to a Roman slave, and scarcely realizing it. Imagine a beam of light penetrating through the ages to this very day! Or, better yet, a light so strong its mirroring never ends. An apt phrasing of this methodology was expressed by its perfect exemplar, just prior to Epictetus: "And I, if I be lifted up from the earth, will draw all men unto me."[2]

True, as Thomas à Kempis stated, neither you nor I can make of ourselves what we wish to be. However, we can march in the right direction. *Thanks to the slave who freed himself!*

---
[1] Liberal Arts Press, The Bobbs-Merrill Company, Indianapolis, 1948.
[2] *John* 12:32.

11

FLOWERS: EMBLEMS OF HUMAN FLOWERING

> *Stars of earth, these golden flowers; emblems of our own great resurrection; emblems of the bright and better land.*
> **—LONGFELLOW**

Recently, one of the most brilliant economists and freedom devotees known to me asked, "Why is it that ever so many people love flowers?" I have loved flowers since childhood, but never, during my 81 years, have I pondered the reason why.

Longfellow finds a poetic correlation between flowers and freedom: the unfolding of a flower into full bloom is symbolic of the evolvement of the human person, under freedom, to his full potential. If more individuals were to realize *why* they love flowers, it is likely that they might grasp why they should love freedom. This thought deserves some exploration, at least for myself, for my friend who asked the question, and perhaps for a few others.

A fortunate coincidence which some persons experience: A moment after completing the above the April 1979 issue of *Natural History* was placed on my desk. Lo and behold, the lead article is entitled, "The Pasqueflower," by Holmes Rolston, III, who teaches philosophy and environmental ethics at Colorado State University. Not only is this a masterpiece of nature writing, but it sheds light on the query as to why so many love flowers.

The author tells of hiking a meadow in the foothills of the Rockies just after the equinox, seeing thousands of this beautiful flower in its finest bloom—an experience I had many years ago in Colorado: Wrote Professor Rolston:

> Earliest among the rites of the western spring is the blossoming of the pasqueflower which . . . precedes by a month the rest of the vernal flora. Its precocious beauty accounts for its name, a flower of the *Pasque,* Easter, and its loveliness, size and season led Aldo Leopold to write, "the chance to find a pasqueflower is as inalienable as free speech."[1]

The more beauty one sees in a flower, the more he or she loves it. The more one understands free speech, freedom of choice and the like, the more he or she loves freedom. There is a correlation here that cannot be dismissed. More by our author:

> . . . such a brave flower can help us ponder what it means to live in and against the wild. So I venture here to let the meeting of it take a philosophical turn.

---

[1]This and subsequent passages are reprinted with permission from *Natural History Magazine,* April, 1979. Copyright © the American Museum of Natural History, 1979.

Flowers: Emblems of Human Flowering   57

"Flowering" touches values so soon, this biological phenomenon becomes a metaphor *for all the striving toward fruition* that characterizes the psychological, intellectual, cultural, and even the spiritual levels of life.

Whatever its antiquity, we might first think, that association has no natural basis; it is entirely fictional. But we later find connections that are so fundamental . . . that we are hardly aware of them.

Awareness! Reflect on the bountiful wonders of freedom. Most Americans take these blessings for granted and have lost all awareness of their origin. Result? No more is required of them to preserve freedom than to preserve the air they breathe! The pasqueflower has this and more lessons for mankind:

Perhaps it may not be so fanciful but rather entirely realistic that this pasqueflower should in its limited and natural way come to serve as a symbol for what Jesus in his unlimited, supernatural way represents to the Christian mind, a hint of *the release of life from the powers that would suppress it.*

For longer than we can remember flowers have been flung up to argue against the forces of violence. . . . This is why it is liberating to find the pasqueflower bearing with beauty the winds of March.

And this is why it is that freedom argues against violence and, thus, liberates mankind. Thanks, Professor Rolston!

Henry Wadsworth Longfellow, born 126 years before Professor Rolston, had similar views, the difference being in phrasing, the latter referring to flowers as "symbols," the former as "emblems." An emblem? Says the dictionary: "allegorically suggesting some moral truth."

In the politico-economic realm, what greater moral truth than our—America's—"great resurrection" from the autocracies that prevailed prior to 1776! Flowers are, indeed, the symbols, the emblems of the "bright and better land." *Freedom shall bloom again!*

Some decades ago it was scientifically demonstrated that flowers grow much better among individuals who love them than among those who are indifferent. Likewise, freedom reigns among those who love this ideal way of life and is impossible where indifference prevails.

I now know why some of us love flowers. They symbolize and are emblems of human flowering—freedom to act creatively as we please. Wrote Goethe: "We are shaped and fashioned by what we love."

Let us love flowers and freedom!

12

THE BLESSINGS OF MORAL OBLIGATIONS

What do I owe to my times, to my country, to my neighbors, to my friends? Such are the questions which a virtuous man ought often to ask himself.
—**JOHANN KASPER LAVATER**

Obligations are of numerous kinds, ranging from the payment of debts, to the keeping of promises and contracts, to moral responsibility or, as the English poet, William Wordsworth, phrased it, "stern daughter of the voice of God."

However defined, obligations are rarely thought of as blessings. My thesis is that moral responsibility, if it is truly a blessing in disguise, ought then to be exposed—pull that veil away! Why? Because an awareness of our blessings is part and parcel of the good life.

Charles Dickens (1812-70), English novelist, sheds light: "Reflect upon your present blessings, of which every man has many; not on your past misfortunes, of which all men have some." Here, then, are some of my reflections on present blessings and past misfortunes and their consequences.

In 1965 during a discussion session at a FEE Seminar in Missouri, a deeply religious individual asked, "What is the significance of the Commandment, 'Thou shalt not covet'?" Never having pondered that one before, I gave him what is a correct answer to many questions, "I do not know." However, the query kept nagging at me—a challenge that wouldn't down.

After considerable reflection, I realized that this Commandment—the tenth—is more important than all but the first. Covetousness—envy—lies at the root of stealing, killing, bearing false witness and many other evils. My conclusion: To the extent that the souls of Americans are cleansed of covetousness, to that extent will we be graced with stalwart, righteous citizens. The formula for ridding ourselves of these traits? *Count our blessings!*

As related to this thesis, there is an attitude that dominates thinking and another that could become dominant. Voltaire expressed my views: "The longer we dwell on our misfortunes, the greater is their power to *harm* us." Just as obvious: "The longer we dwell on our blessings, the greater is their power to *improve* us."

As to the first attitude, one should, by all means, be keenly aware of the misfortunes which beset society. Properly assessed, they are steppingstones to truth—blessings in disguise.

Learn the wrong, to find the right!

Voltaire, however, had in mind the common attitude he

observed in his time—two centuries ago—which is precisely what we observe in the U.S.A. today: citizens by the millions dwelling *only* on the countless misfortunes. The result of this myopic, unperceptive, shortsighted view? Ruled by pessimism, hopelessness, despair, such persons become crepehangers, doubting Thomases, worrywarts.

These people not only do irreparable harm to their own lives but a disservice to the rest of us and, may I add, to the cause of human liberty. No truth was ever advanced by dwelling only on man-made misfortunes—those sad consequences of ignorance or half-truths or outright lies!

Turn now from the negative to the positive, from dwelling on our misfortunes to dwelling on our blessings, from looking hellward to peering heavenward, from that which harms to that which improves. If enough of us do this our countrymen *will know* what precious blessings are theirs, and which no other people on earth enjoy. Too high an aspiration? A bit of reflection will easily replace misery with joy, forlornness with hopefulness.

Conceded, no person will ever count all of his or her blessings. The human being does not exist who can count that far—our blessings border on the Infinite. Every heartbeat is a blessing, as is every breath, all discoveries, inventions, insights, intuitive flashes that have advanced truth and human welfare since the dawn of consciousness. So numerous, they stagger the imagination—delightfully!

The Swiss preacher and theological writer, Johann Kasper Lavater (1741-1801), posed several questions which a virtuous person should often ask. Why virtuous individuals and not everyone? Only those having a sense of moral obligations are capable of asking what they owe to their times, to their neighbors, to their country, to their friends. Those not so graced have the order reversed, namely, insisting on what their country and others owe them.

Looking to the future, will our blessings multiply or will they dwindle and await another renaissance in the near or distant future? The answer, it seems, depends on how well some of us answer the questions above posed. Perhaps the best any of us can do—no one knowing the perfect answers—is to share our thoughts with each other. I owe you mine; you owe me yours.

What do I owe to my time?

As much *growth* in awareness, perception, consciousness as is within my potentiality.

- We always have time enough if we but use it aright.
  —*Goethe*

- Time well employed is Satan's deadliest foe; it leaves no opening for the lurking fiend. —*Carlos Wilcox*

- As if you could kill time without injuring eternity!
  —*Henry David Thoreau*

- Doest thou love life? Then do not squander time, for it is the stuff life is made of. —*Benjamin Franklin*

- Example is the school of mankind. They will learn at no other. —*Edmund Burke*

There is more time to do the worthwhile things in life than anyone will ever discover how to use. I owe to my time the avoidance of trivia, the constant striving to set a better example.

What do I owe to my country?

First is an understanding of the most important of all

The Blessings of Moral Obligations

politico-economic facts, namely, that our rights to life and livelihood are endowed by the Creator and not by government. Second, an ability to explain this *essence of Americanism* with such clarity that others may become aware of the moral principles that made America great.

What do I owe to my neighbors and friends?

The best answer was pronounced centuries ago in both the Old and New Testaments: *Love thy neighbor as thyself.* The English author, Francis Quarles (1592-1644), nicely embellished this truth: "If thou neglectest thy love to thy neighbor, in vain thou professest thy love to God; for by thy love to God, the love of thy neighbor is begotten, and by the love of thy neighbor, thy love to God is nourished."

Love is, in a sense, retroactive brotherhood. Extend it to neighbors or friends or whoever with no thought beyond "It is more blessed to give than to receive." With this attitude, the recipients will, more than likely, do the same and thou wilt be blest in thy giving.

High among the moral obligations, particularly when coercion—socialism—threatens our future, is the understanding and sharing of freedom principles, ideas and ideals.

Through my lectures and other contacts in 22 foreign nations and 48 of our states during the past 34 years, I have gained numerous good friends—good devotees of freedom—teachable as each of us should be. These individuals are among my countless blessings—each and everyone! The Third Beatitude, when translated aright, reads: *The teachable shall inherit the earth!*

13

TWIN VIRTUES: RESPONSIBLE AND RESPONSIVE

> *It is easy to dodge responsibilities, but we cannot dodge the consequences of dodging our responsibilities.*
> —JOSIAH C. STAMP

This English economist and financier (1880-1941) was unable to dodge the consequence of those who were dodging their responsibilities. The consequence? This outstanding man was killed by one of Hitler's bombs dropped on England. And it is difficult, if not impossible, to find a man in all history who dodged responsibilities more than that infamous Nazi. While Josiah Stamp did not foresee the cause of his demise, he foresaw the relationship between individual responsibility and the good life!

Reflection on the twin virtues of "responsible and responsive" brings to mind an observation of Plato: "Virtue is free, and as a man honors or dishonors her he will have more or less of her; the responsibility is with the chooser."

Twin Virtues: Responsible and Responsive 65

There's no doubt that more people choose to dishonor than choose to honor the virtue of being responsible. And the cause, more often than not, is their unawareness that being self-responsible is a virtue. Here is a comical dialogue that dramatizes the point:

Employer: "For this job we want a responsible man."
Applicant: "Then you want me. Everywhere I've worked, when something went wrong they said I was responsible."

Regardless of how far any country has slumped into dictatorship, there always have been a few citizens graced with self-responsibility and self-reliance—societal saviors! Were this not the case, the entire citizenry would consist of man-like puppets, manipulated by a Hitler, a Stalin, or some other of that disgraceful type. Obviously, all would perish!

Americans have had and do have many responsible citizens emerging from countless varieties of political enslavement. There may be no better illustration than one who rose out of our deplorable Negro slavery: Booker T. Washington (1856-1915). His mother was a mulatto slave on a plantation, his father a white man. When old enough, Booker worked in salt furnaces and coal mines. This responsible Negro kept going up the ladder of achievement and became a remarkable educator, organizing a school for Negroes—Tuskegee Institute. He was a first-rate freedom devotee, and was also regarded as one of the greatest speakers of his time.

Did Booker T. Washington's responsibility result in responsiveness? A single example: One of his students, George Washington Carver (1864-1943) became another free market exponent. He gained international fame in agricultural research, opening opportunities for ever so many in the South, black as well as white. The solid achievements of men like Washington and Carver have done more to lower the barriers of discrimination and prejudice than the passage of laws and the rhetoric of agitators.

The above, by itself, makes the case for the twin virtues of responsible and responsive. However, this important subject deserves more reflection.

Wrote William Ernest Hocking: "You can only make men free when they are inwardly bound by their own sense of responsibility." According to G. K. Chesterton: "It isn't that Christianity has been tried and found wanting. It has been tried and found difficult and all but abandoned." A similar observation can be made about freedom. It isn't that freedom has been tried and found wanting. Rather, it has been tried and found to require responsibility for self, whereupon it has been abandoned by millions of Americans. They give in to socialistic promises, "to each according to need."

A good friend, Verna Hall, has caused numerous individuals to be liberated from their weakness—*responsive* to a well-phrased truth: "To the extent that an individual turns the responsibility for self over to another or allows government to take it away, *to that extent is the very essence of one's being removed.*" Hocking, the Harvard philosopher of a generation ago, had he read this wisdom, would have been proud of our friend's emphasis on responsibility and the responsive results thereof.

Every person who strives for excellence in life should put his high goals just out of reach. The wise words of an

American Episcopal Bishop, Phillips Brooks (1835-93), provide one such goal: "Be such a man, and live such a life, that if every man were such as you, and every life a life like yours, this earth would be God's Paradise."

Surely, this Bishop did not mean that we should all be alike, but that others should be similar to you or me in only one respect: in ardently striving for virtue. True, we finite mortals cannot come close to Infinite Consciousness—God's Paradise—but each of us can aim his life in that direction. If our striving be sufficiently excellent, we become exemplars of righteousness. "Example is the school of mankind. They will learn at no other."

Josiah Stamp and numerous others foresaw the relation between responsibility and the good life—a mode of living where each is free to act creatively as he pleases. More of us than now must attain an attractive exemplarity as related to this virtue if we are to be blest with a return to freedom. Why is this a *must?* Where self-responsibility is absent, power mongers fill the thoughtless gap; they run our lives. It is either one or the other. Thank, heaven, we are free to choose.

Those of us who choose freedom must follow the counsel of Abraham Lincoln: "You can't escape the responsibility of tomorrow by evading it today." Act now! This virtue educates and causes its practitioners to be attractive. Thus it gives birth to its twin, responsiveness.

Daniel Webster added his counsel: "The most important thought I have ever had was that of *my individual responsibility to God.*" This is righteousness. Reflect on how responsive countless citizens have been to this outstanding statesman!

To paraphrase a great thinker: Freedom will not descend to Americans; we must raise ourselves to freedom. It is a priceless blessing that must be earned before it can be enjoyed.

The earning of freedom is one of the greatest of all earthly joys!

14

TO ACQUIRE? DESIRE AND ASPIRE!

> *Lord, grant me that I may always desire more than I can accomplish.* —**MICHELANGELO**

The use of the word "acquire," in this little essay, does not relate to such infamous ambitions as fame, popularity, political or any kind of coercive power over others. Rather, the reference is, as Michelangelo implies, what the Lord would have us do. The instruction is recorded in Matthew 6:33: "But seek ye first the Kingdom of God and his Righteousness [Truth] and all these things [material well-being] shall be added unto you." Here is how C. S. Lewis phrased the above: "Aim at Heaven [Truth] and we will get earth [material well-being] thrown in. Aim at earth and we will get neither."

Ever so many people have the amassing of wealth as life's sole ambition. Wrong, in my view! How should we assess our material well-being? Caleb C. Colton gave us an appropriate guideline: "If you would take your possessions into the life to come, *convert them into good deeds.*" Briefly, our earthly moments should be devoted to a growth in consciousness which lives on personally and eternally—good deed number one!

The famous Italian, Michelangelo (1475-1546), was not only one of the world's greatest painters of all time but also a genius as a sculptor, architect and poet. Devotion to his earthly callings? Observe his painting on the ceiling of the Sistine Chapel in Rome, a task at which he spent 37 years!

Most people, when they attain some minor ambition, be it infamous or laudable, drop by the wayside—life's mission accomplished; desire at an end; aspiration in the past tense! Growth in consciousness? None! In this respect, they become stunted men and women—intellectual dwarfs. Emulate them not!

Seldom in all history do we find an individual with the numerous and varied skills of a Michelangelo—on the topmost rungs of the ladder of accomplishment. Yet his prayer was to desire ever more and more; perpetual growth during his mortal moments was the goal to which he aspired. Why emulate his kind? It is their way of life that gives birth to the freedom way of life—what the Lord would have us do.

Richard Cabot, M.D. (1868-1939), teacher of social ethics at Harvard Medical School, and Chief of Staff at Massachusetts General Hospital for many years, beautifully phrased the way freedom works its wonders and its Source:

> When you say to me, "Thank you," remember I could not have done for you what I did, had it not been for what hundreds of other people have done for me. Neither could

To Acquire? Desire and Aspire!

they have done for me what they did, had it not been for the thousands of other people who had done for them. And so the thing goes on *in infinite time and space;* and therefore when you say, "thank you," you really mean to say, "Thank you, God."

Thus it is that our gratitude for the blessings of freedom should be extended to Infinite Consciousness!

Let's suppose that these thoughts I am trying to put together—thoughts which I have borrowed from many people —turn out to be useful to you. I should then be as thankful to you for accepting them as you are thankful to me for offering such thoughts.

Reflect on my dependency not only on the thoughts of others but on the thousands of things they do for me. They grow my food and prepare much of it; build and heat and light my home; make my clothes, on and on endlessly, even providing the pen with which this is written. Result? I am free to pursue that object in life which most intrigues me: aspiring to a better understanding and exposition of freedom!

Here are a few more thoughts—put into my own phrasing—borrowed from *Inherit The Earth* by N. J. Berrill, a man who has held numerous notable positions, including Professor of Zoology at McGill University.[1] I owe him a "Thank you" for offering his thoughts and he owes me and others the same for using them.

Everyone above the moronic level entertains some thoughts—good, bad and indifferent. However, unless these are activated—spelled out and explained—they are ephem-

---
[1] Dodd, Mead & Co., New York (1966).

eral, evanescent and, as dreams. Unused ideas are but nothings in the past tense. The message for those of us who love liberty?

Hide not your light under a bushel; do not keep thoughts to yourself. Instead, let each one achieve such excellence in words and deed that others will not only seek his tutorship but, hopefully, strive to outdo him. Share! Adhere to the law of attraction!

Our universe is creative at all levels—from tiny atoms, to sunshine, to immeasurable galaxies ever moving further and further into outer space. We humans are an integral, small but significant part thereof but we differ from other parts as related to creativity. Using the word God as the symbol of Creation, an atom, for instance, is God-created. It performs in accord with its God-given nature, having no more power to choose than does the moon. How does man, while also God-created, differ? My associate, Reverend E. A. Opitz, gives an excellent answer:

> Man transcends nature and is gifted with a novel kind of freedom of choice. Here at last is a creature so detached from the instinctual controls that guide animals that he can defy the laws of his being. The other orders of Creation—birds, beasts, insects—possess built-in servomechanisms which give them all the answers they need. But man has not been given the answers; before our eyes the Creator has poised a question mark and the answers are ours to work out. This is our freedom, and also our peril. . . . Man's freedom is so radical that he can deny his own nature—he can deny his Maker.

Let us choose wisely and well in the ongoing creative task

To Acquire? Desire and Aspire!   73

of improving our minds. The freedom way of life is to that extent self-made.

Here is a direct quote from Professor Berrill's book:

> And potentialities mean not just skills, but the full range of the capacities for sensing, wondering, learning, understanding, loving, and *aspiring*. In this light, the ultimate goal of the educational system is *to shift to the individual the burden of pursuing his own education.* (Italics added)

How few there are who grasp Berrill's important point that the personal seeking of truth from sources past and present—private education—is the way to enlightenment.

Another direct quote from Professor Berrill:

> A so-called average individual is in a dignified position upon a pinnacle.... He needs to know that whether his gifts are large or small *they are his own,* that he sees the world around him in a somewhat different way than has ever been seen before. And he needs to know that when all minds are uncommon the most uncommon may have by far the most to tell, and that *the greater the minds the greater the differences.* As the brain has grown, the differences between one and another are magnified accordingly. When visual regions reach their peak, *a Michelangelo* can arise creating shape and color from solid forms. When vision combines with the sense and memory of dynamic action you get a Leonardo da Vinci. *These are uncommon giants ... but they are giants who grew out of the so-called common stock of a multitude of uncommon individuals.* (Italics added).

Those of us not crowned with power—voted or coercively grabbed—are uncommon individuals, no two remotely alike. Our potentialities? Fritz Kunkel, the eminent psychologist, revealed what is a secret to most people: *"Immense hidden powers* lurk in the unconscious of the most common man—indeed, of all people without exception.''

True, we will not, because of our differences, ever be a Michelangelo, Leonardo da Vinci, Edison or a duplicate of anyone else. But we can become uncommon giants—individuals contributing to human evolution.

If our differences are to grow and flow to the advantage of all, freedom must prevail—an absolute necessity! And to aspire toward this glorious end, we can, in one respect, be like the great Michelangelo: *Lord, grant me that I may always desire more than I can accomplish.*

15

BELIEVE IN THIS MIRACLE: FREEDOM

The practical effect of a belief is the real test of its soundness.
—**J. A. FROUDE**

What is a miracle? "It is," says the dictionary, "an event or action that apparently contradicts known scientific laws and is hence thought to be due to supernatural causes especially to an act of God." Creation!

Why do so few approve, accept and abide by the freedom way of life? A confession: I, along with many others, have been saying, "It's so difficult to explain." The truth as I now see it? *No one can or ever will be able to explain this miracle!* Were clear, lucid and persuasive explanation a requirement, some one or more of us would need to understand and explain every facet of human action—creation at the human level. No individual is or ever has been graced with such wisdom. Nor is such omniscience necessary for a belief in freedom.

Everything in Creation, including every form of life—no exception—is a miracle when viewed aright. However, one will seldom find a recording among famous intellectuals—past or present—who will agree with this statement. One notable exception was an English divine, Robert South (1634-1716): "A miracle is a work *exceeding the power of any created agent,* consequently being an effect of the divine omnipotence."

The preponderance of people who deny the reality of anything beyond their capacity to explain may be a blessing in disguise. This is one of several reasons why so many individuals have looked upon freedom, not as a miracle, but as an explainable way of life. Being unable to explain it themselves and knowing of no one who can, it is held in far less esteem than socialism which can be and is easier to explain than a zero.

All but a few are blind to freedom's miracles. Thomas Alva Edison, perhaps the greatest inventive genius of all time, gave us one explanation for this blindness: "No one knows more than a millionth of one per cent of anything." This, of course, is a figure of speech. He could have said a billionth or trillionth of one per cent. Compared to Infinite Consciousness, finite man is no more than a mere speck in Creation's Domain. Grasping this point—the more one knows the more awareness of how little he knows—is the beginning of such wisdom as is within mortal man's domain.

There are reasons galore as to why freedom is not believed to be a miracle. Here is one: Our everyday life is

Believe in this Miracle: Freedom 77

crowded with miracles, so many that they have become commonplace. No one "contradicts" them. My telephone is an example. I can send my voice around the earth at the speed of light—in a fraction of a second. While few will think of this recent phenomenon as a miracle, I have never heard anyone say it is not. No contradiction! During the past few decades millions of miracles, ranging from penicillin to jet airplanes, are taken for granted, accepted as are the miracles of nature, be they blades of grass or giant oaks.

Froude, the English historian (1818-94) wrote: "The practical effect of a belief is the real test of its soundness." Is it practical to believe in the unexplainable miracle, freedom? The answer is an unequivocal *"Yes"!* Why? Because the individual's freedom to act creatively as he pleases is materially, morally and spiritually *sound*.

At our down-to-earth level, more miracles than anyone can count result from freedom, the greatest demonstration in all history being the American miracle!

There is one detail that should be explainable but no one to my knowledge has phrased it well enough for effective communication: it has to do with individual differences. Let us find a way to put these facts into understandable terms: No two of us are remotely alike. Indeed, no one individual is the same now as he or she was a moment ago. All is change now and forever. When our tiny bits of expertise are free to flow, they configurate. As drops of water make an ocean, so do these bits make the miracle.

Here are some final thoughts gleaned from that brilliant Frenchman, Alexis de Tocqueville (1805-1859). But first for some background. During the middle years of the last century, numerous governments sent commissions to the

U.S.A. to find out why our success and their failures. All of them went home with the wrong answers. Tocqueville, by himself, made the all important discovery:

> I sought for the greatness and genius of America in fertile fields and boundless forests; it was not there. I sought for it in her institutions of learning; it was not there. I sought for it in her matchless Constitution and democratic congress; it was not there. Not until I went to the churches of America and found them aflame with righteousness did I understand the greatness and genius of America. *America is great because America is good. When America ceases to be good, America will cease to be great.*

A few other thoughts by Tocqueville which lend credence to this thesis:

> The soil is productive less by reason of its natural fertility than because the people tilling it are free.
>
> In fact, those who prize freedom only for the material benefits it offers have never kept it long.
>
> For only in countries where it reigns can a man speak, live and breathe freely. . . . The man who asks of freedom anything other than itself is born to be a slave.
>
> Some nations have freedom in the blood and are ready to face the greatest perils and hardships in its defense. . . . Other nations, once they have grown prosperous, lose interest in freedom and let it be snatched from them without lifting a hand to defend it, lest they should endanger thus the comforts that, in fact, *they owe to it alone*. It is easy to see that what is lacking in such nations is a genuine love of freedom, that lofty aspiration which (I

confess) *defies analysis. For it* [freedom's miracles] *is something one must feel and logic has no part in it.*[1]

Wrote Charles F. Kettering: "Logic is an organized way of going wrong with confidence." This inventive genius passed away before discovering why grass is green. Why is it that no one can answer this question? A blade of grass is no more nor less a miracle than freedom itself. Boss Kettering gave to freedom devotees a brilliant formula: "Nothing ever built arose to touch the skies unless some man dreamed that it should, some man *believed* that it could, and some man willed that it must."

Believe in our miracle and freedom will rise again!

---

[1] These are excerpts from Tocqueville's book, *The Old Regime and The French Revolution*.

16

THE GLORY OF OUR WORLDS GALORE

Oh, what a glory doth this world put on, for him who with a fervent heart goes forth under the bright and glorious sky, and looks on duties well performed, and days well spent. **—LONGFELLOW**

Among the numerous definitions of "worlds" is "individual experience." Each individual who inhabits this earth has varying experiences every day of mortal life, from which are fashioned his or her countless worlds. Life provides us with an opportunity to grow, or as Henry Ward Beecher put it, "The world is God's workshop for making men." Let's reflect on how this "workshop world" idea *makes* men when duties are well performed, and days well spent.

I like Beecher's "the world is God's workshop for making men." It suggests that as a man chooses wisely or foolishly, he succeeds or fails, flourishes or withers, lives or dies. In this sense, God's world comes down to the infinitely vari-

The Glory of Our Worlds Galore

able worlds of "individual experience," and from that infinite variety evolve better persons—obviously, the first vital step to a better world. The key to such evolution is freedom, the opportunity to rise or to fall, depending on one's choices and actions. But the right or the wrong of a given action is judged not according to the human whim of the moment but by the unwavering moral standards of Creation, Nature, God.

Many years ago a good friend of our efforts asked, "I don't have to believe in God to believe in freedom do I?" My reply: "No, you do not have to believe in God to believe in freedom. But if no one believed in God there would be no freedom." As explained in another chapter, freedom would be impossible were everyone atheists—nothing but chaos!

The term "God" has only the vaguest of connotations for the average person. It is widely believed, for example, that "God" is "The *Man* Upstairs"—an anthropomorphic concept. On the other hand, many, throughout the ages, have used "God"—and rightly so—to symbolize the Infinite Being—beyond our concepts and images. No person has ever known *what* Being is, only *that* It is. Creation—Infinite Consciousness—may be the best term to label the indescribable. Once this thought be grasped, we mortals recognize—and properly—our infinitesimal relation to the Infinite: "approaching zero!"

Short of a recognition of mankind's near-zero position, a horrible notion takes over, one that has plagued humanity throughout recorded history: *Man* (with a capital M!) *is the source of all creativity*. There is no greater blockage to evolution than this!

But if evolution is to grace our lives, as is our destiny, it will be founded on an intellectual revolution: a politico-economic enlightenment on the part of only a few. Why a few? Every good movement in all history has been led by an infinitesimal minority—a handful, so to speak. A near-zero number understanding and explaining man's near-zero position relative to Creation, Nature, God!

No individual, past or present, ever has or ever will *program progress!* Why this assertion? All humans are near zeros relative to Creation, Nature, God. Socrates, admittedly wise, could no more contrive a way to send the human voice around our earth in a fraction of a second than I can compose Grand Opera or take John Wayne's place as an actor. Comparable limitations apply to all who live or ever will! A recognition of this fact on the part of a few is the first step if mankind is to enjoy progress.

The second step? A deep and abiding faith in a politico-economic phenomenon: only in the freedom of everyone to act creatively can we who know next to nothing—mere seedlings—assure progress.

Why is this faith and not knowledge? I know that the sun shines but not why it does; that grass is green but not why it is. There are millions of phenomena—flowerings of Creation at the human level. When first appearing—a flying machine, for instance—they are applauded. But when advanced to the 747 jet, they become commonplace to the masses, appreciation deadened—no more cheers as to the wonders of freedom, the source of which is Creation. This brings to mind two contrasting verses, author unknown:

Fueled by a million man-made wings of fire,
The rocket tore through the sky. . . .
And everyone cheered.

The Glory of Our Worlds Galore

> Fueled only by a thought from God,
> The seedling urged its way through the thickness of black.
> And as it pierced the heavy ceiling of the soil
> And launched itself up into outer space. . . .
> No one even clapped.

Great oaks from little acorns grow. Similarly, tiny bits of expertise grow—providing they are free to flow and configurate. It is now appropriate to reflect upon the obstacles to the free, unobstructed flowing of creative human energy.

The first obstacle is failure to grow, wasting away—atrophy. The cause? Doubtless, most of the reasons are unknown. An *unawareness* of Creation's workshop takes first place, for *It* is *The Source* of all creativity.

The result of this unawareness? The millions cursed with this fogginess mistakenly regard themselves as source. They accept the faulty premise that whatever goes on in the universe originates with finite mortals. Errors multiply and result in disappointments, fears for the future, unhappiness. Their worlds are featured with woes!

"Thinking" in this manner—the problems of mankind on *their* shoulders—they, in their intellectual infancy, seek to become self-appointed, politico-economic trouble shooters. A vast majority of our 16,000,000 elected and appointed government officials fall into this ignoble category; but they merely reflect the know-it-all-ness of most citizens. Such persons, in or out of office, have a "cure" for every real or presumed ill. When their nostrums fail to work, they gloomily predict a future which, as they see it, is fraught with calamity. They become pessimists—no faith, none whatsoever, in a turnabout. Unhappy souls who multiply our difficulties!

Freedom—specialization in goods, services, ideas freely flowing—results in an unexpected, unaccustomed wealth. Merely reflect upon how little any of us do in exchange for the enormous bounties we receive! Our meager contribution relative to reward comes so close to approximating something-for-nothing that most people, failing to grasp this phenomenon, miss its evolutionary purpose: *Growth!* Such individuals, therefore, take it easy, cease to strive, look forward to retirement. Result? Atrophy! When "easy come" prosperity is used as an excuse to escape from life, no latent talents are released, and thus, wealth may be destructive.

Specialization, if appraised aright, is an important stepping stone—providing we take advantage of its *unforeseen* potentialities. The real purpose of wealth is to free us from the laborious chores of our predecessors—chopping our own wood, growing our own food, traveling by horse and buggy, and so on. Living in a prosperous society makes it possible for each of us to devote ourselves to personal evolution—to come up with one new understanding after another.

In summary, the right or wrong of a given action should always be judged, not according to any human whim of this or any future moment, but by the unwavering moral standards of Creation, Nature, God! When thus judged, we can, indeed, *glory in our worlds galore!*

17

THE SOURCE OF WISDOM

There is one person that is wiser than anybody, and that is everybody. **—TALLEYRAND**

The above observation by Talleyrand (1754-1838), a French cardinal, might easily be misinterpreted. A man of his faith would be the first to agree that the initial source of all human wisdom is Infinite Consciousness—Creation. Obviously, he was referring to such wisdom as exists among finite humans. And, here again, he might be misunderstood. Assuredly, he did not mean by "everybody," a mere body count of the many billions who have inhabited or presently inhabit this earth. That would not make sense and Talleyrand was a sensible person. What then?

The "everybody" to whom he referred were those individuals who are not "nobodies"—an amputation which dramatically reduces the number of "everybodies!" Who are these "nobodies," as related to the source of wisdom? They are the millions who have all sorts of aims other than wisdom. A few samplings:

- The seekers of political power, that they may run the lives of others.
- The seekers of fame, fortune, and notoriety.
- The seekers of shorter hours, time off, vacations, retirement.
- The seekers of countless something-for-nothing schemes, that is, living off productive citizens: food stamps, social security and the like.
- The seekers of special privileges, ranging from rent control to embargoes to many other non-competitive devices.
- All who support any phase of the planned economy and the welfare state.

The wisdom here under discussion refers not only to spiritual and moral insight; it refers also to the intuitions that underlie the laws of science, and the technological breakthroughs on which our increasing prosperity depends. It is fairly obvious, then, that we "nobodies" are not the source of wisdom—although we are its beneficiaries. What about the "everybodies?" Not a one of them thinks of himself as *the* source. Possessing an understanding of freedom, and having faith in the way freedom works its wonders, they do not even regard themselves as *a* source, but rather as transmitters. In short, well over 99 per cent of our "everybodies" go through life as sources of wisdom—*unknowingly!*

How shall we account for this? To the extent that peaceful persons are not coerced, in that same measure do free actions prevail, talents emerge. Wrote Edmund Burke: "As to great and commanding talents, they are the gifts of providence in some way *unknown* to us. They rise where they are least expected."

Great and commanding talents are, indeed, the gifts of Providence. Here is a great truth by Emerson which I have used numerous times: "We lie in the lap of immense intelligence which makes us receivers of its truth and organs of its activities. When we discern justice, when we discern truth, we do nothing of ourselves, but allow a passage of its beams."

Socrates was acclaimed as the wisest of men, but he himself claimed only that he was aware of the extent of his own ignorance. He did not profess to be the source of any wisdom, but referred to himself as a mere "philosophical midwife." As to the Immense Intelligence—God, Infinite Consciousness—Socrates merely tried to allow a passage of its beams. By not obstructing the truth, he did succeed in receiving messages from the Divine Source. He became one of the "everybodies," perhaps more so than any other known to me. He received, and what he was given, he shared.

Socrates *knew* the Source of such wisdom as graced his life, and by tapping it he benefited every one of us. Wisdom, then, might flow through us, and we, too, might experience discoveries, inventions, little flashes of insight and the like. The number of these blessings are countless in any given day. Talents galore! They account in no small measure for the progress that our rapidly growing socialism has not yet destroyed.

However, an additional talent must be achieved if we are to avoid a socialistic disaster: a recognition of *The Source*. It is unlikely that you or I will attain a Socratic level, but we can come to recognize, as did he, that we are intermediaries—receivers of ideas from *The Source*—and, by so doing, achieve the required talent: receiving and sharing. We then become a *knowing* "everybody," a source of attraction, the best contribution we can make to the dismissal of socialistic nonsense.

Assume that we move in the right direction, that success attends our efforts, that socialism fades away and freedom returns to grace our lives. Will we then be relieved of further effort? Quite the opposite! The further we travel the righteous road, the steeper and more difficult it becomes. The more we advance, emerge, the more each individual differs from his fellows. Variation! The more varied, the more interdependent, that is, the more do we live by voluntary exchanges of the fruits of each other's specialized labor. What is the binding quality required, and absolute source of wisdom? It is an *ever-improving morality!*

Moral philosophy is the study of right and wrong, good and evil, better and worse. Economics is the study of what's right in overcoming scarcity. Moreover, the two are inseparable. The latter cannot be achieved except as the former is improved.

Wrote Montaigne: "The principal office of wisdom is to distinguish good and evil."

The source of wisdom is discovering and abiding by the good!

18

THE KEYS TO GREATNESS

> *Subtract from the great man all that he owes to opportunity, all that he owes to chance, and all that he has gained by the wisdom of his friends and the folly of his enemies, and the giant will often be seen to be a pigmy.*
> **—CALEB C. COLTON**

The above is an excellent listing of the self-deceptions and oversights which may prevent the ordinary person from achieving his potential stature, or may cause him to lapse into what Colton describes as a "pigmy" condition. An appropriate phrase for these latter, in our time, might be "mental midgets."

Why is it that most people never come close to realizing their potentialities—becoming great? It is an unawareness of the munificent gifts that can be theirs for nothing more than self-discovery. Sir Isaac Newton (1642-1727), a distinguished scientist and philosopher, gave to posterity the key talent: "If I have ever made any valuable discoveries, it has been owing more to *patient attention,* than to any other talent." So let us give patient attention to the keys suggested by the English clergyman, Caleb Colton (1780-1832).

All that he owes to opportunity. Reflect on the countless opportunities that have opened to all of us and for a simple reason: the freedom—now threatened—to act creatively as we please. Take a single instance among millions: the invention of the telephone. No one can make a fair guess as to the number of individuals to whom this gives employment. It is ever so many times more than the number of people who work for the telephone companies around the world. Included are the makers of the instruments, erectors of poles and the foresters thereof, producers of wire, printers of telephone books, and so on.

My great-grandfather had no such opportunity. Nor did he have an opportunity to work in automobile production or in its many subsidiary industries. Nor in a million other entrepreneurial adventures!

Suppose this ancestor of mine, the first settler in Shiawassee County, Michigan, had been able to hear me talk about my air travel for the past 60 years. He would have accused me of telling fairy tales. Suppose I told him about a 747 jet with its 5,000,000 parts—although no person on earth knows how to make a single one of them. Think of the immense number of jobs spawned by the aircraft industry, and their enormous variety. Opportunities unlimited, unknown to my great-grandfather.

I have two great-grandchildren. If we keep socialism from destroying freedom, their opportunities will be as astonishing to us as ours would have been to my forefather!

The Keys to Greatness

Margaret Cameron in her book, *The Seven Great Purposes,* brilliantly phrased the point I wish to make: "Give unto each his opportunity to grow and to build for progress. Freedom to strive is the one right inherent in existence, the strong and the weak each following his own purpose, with all his force, to the one great end. *And he who binds and limits his brother's purpose binds himself now and hereafter. But he who extends his brother's opportunity, builds for eternity.*"

All that he owes to chance. Philosophers have interesting and varying views on Chance due, no doubt, to the way the eye is cast. There's a negative side. Thus Thomas Fuller: "He who trusts all things to Chance, makes a Lottery of his Life."

Many side with Voltaire: "Chance is a word void of sense; nothing can exist without cause." All things, from blades of grass to the wisest humans, sprout from a variety of causes—mostly unknown.

There is, however, a sensible side to Chance. Wrote Lord Halifax: "He that leaveth nothing to Chance will do few things ill, but he will do very few things." How limited my own life would be had not countless happenings—the unexpected or Chances—blest my actions. Ever so many can make this same confession.

One of the best statements was written by Terence over 2,000 years ago. This man was born a slave but given his freedom by a Roman Senator. Terence became a great writer of comedy, several of his works well-known to this day. He had good reason to write: "How often things occur by the merest Chance, [his unexpected freedom] which we dared not even hope for."

All that has been gained by the wisdom of his friends. This brings to mind a conversation of 25 years ago. I was seated next to the host of a FEE Seminar at the opening dinner. In the course of our conversation, he remarked, "Since meeting you, Leonard, I have a whole new set of friends." Startling! "What do you mean, Don?" "Before meeting you, those in the fast set were my friends. You interested me in freedom. Now, people like these at this Seminar—freedom devotees—are my friends."

Who are *my* friends? The ones who enlighten me, those individuals—past and present—whom I repeatedly quote, such as Caleb Colton, author of the above observation. These seers—and their number is legion—are graced with more common sense as related to Truth, Righteousness, Freedom than any others known to me. Wrote Samuel Coleridge: "Common sense in an *uncommon degree* is what the world calls wisdom."

Assume that my life had been lived without the bits of wisdom gleaned from others. I couldn't do the multiplication table, or read, or speak more clearly than a chimpanzee.

Move to the level here at issue and imagine that I had not a single friend of my present persuasion. Such phrases as private ownership, free market, limited government wouldn't be in my vocabulary—a politico-economic dunce!

Joseph Story (1779-1845), Associate Justice, U.S. Supreme Court, wrote: "Human wisdom is the aggregate of all human experience, constantly accumulating, selecting and reorganizing its own materials."

The folly of his enemies. I would phrase this final point thus: Subtract from the great man all he might learn from the

The Keys to Greatness

follies of freedom's adversaries—socialists—and this will lower him to a mental midget. If aspiring to true greatness, we will "love our enemies" for the help they give us!

Never, under any circumstances, think of socialists as "enemies." Such derogatory assessments cause them to regard lovers of liberty as enemies and to look upon their own errors as truth. It hardens them in their ways! What then? Dismiss from our talk, writing, even thinking, the "thou fool" folly and proceed *impersonally*—dealing solely with false notions. If we are skillful enough in explaining the fallacy of the "we-can-run-your-life-better-than-you-can" syndrome, they may do a turnabout. Or try silence! Silence, under certain provocations, is truly golden.

Overcoming false notions is an intellectual imperative; they are the steppingstones to truth. Acts of overcoming pave the road to becoming—man's purpose. All history attests to this. Were there no intellectual obstacles—no mishmash, all sublime—there would be no activity above the shoulders. Humanity dying on the vine!

Wrote William Cullen Bryant:
> Truth, crushed to earth, shall rise again,
> Th' eternal years of God are hers;
> But Error, wounded, writhes in vain,
> And dies among his worshippers.

The one great key to greatness? See John 8:32: *And ye shall know the truth, and the truth shall make you free.*

19

LIVING THE GOOD LIFE

Be such a man and live such a life, that if every man were such as you, and every life a life like yours, this earth would be God's Paradise. —**PHILLIPS BROOKS**

The Encyclopedia writes of the Episcopal Bishop, Phillips Brooks (1835-93): "... a gifted preacher and a man of broad and generous sympathies, fine spiritual qualities and unusual charm, he won wide esteem.... The Christmas Hymn, *O Little Town of Bethlehem* was written by him."

Assume that I fervently strive every day of my life to attain the perfection Bishop Brooks suggests—righteousness and perfection in everything my only guideline. Were all on earth to similarly strive, would our world be God's Paradise? An emphatic "No"! Nor, in my view, would the Bishop disagree. A man of his wisdom could have had no more in mind than a lofty goal such as was brilliantly expressed by an Englishman, Philip Chesterfield (1694-1773): "Aim at perfection in everything, though in most things it is unattainable; however, they who aim at it, and persevere, will come much nearer to it, than those whose laziness and despondency make them give it up as unattainable."

With the above as background, it seems appropriate to reflect on the means—thoughts and actions—which will move us in the direction of an unattainable perfection.

Years ago I read a book by a popular college professor in which he argued that competition was antagonistic to cooperation. Away with the former that the latter might prevail! What a fallacy. For the truth is that we compete in order to cooperate!

Example: When the bakers of bread compete in quality and price, it is easy for us consumers to decide whose bread to buy, that is, with which baker we will cooperate. In the absence of competition, all of us would be stranded at the level of "take it, or leave it." When the free and unfettered market prevails, there is a race for excellence. Indeed, even today with all the obstacles—governmental interventions—the game of economic leapfrogging goes on at whirlwind pace.

Senator Clay had this to say before the U.S. Senate in 1832: "Of all human powers operating on the affairs of mankind, none is greater than that of competition." Seven years earlier, W. S. Landor wrote: "Competition is as wholesome in religion as in commerce." Briefly, competition is essential to progress in whatever field of endeavor!

Contrary to liberal mythology, competition is as necessary to intellectual, moral and spritual growth as it is to an abundance of goods and services. In the absence of competition, cooperation in learning and explaining freedom is impossible. Leapfrogging—out-doing each other—is a procedure which we must believe in and practice.

When it comes to acquiring goods and services, we have two guidelines: (1) our desire for this or that and (2) the price. When desire exceeds the price, we buy; when the price is too high for our desire, no transaction.

Now for an unorthodox question: Do prices furnish a clue as to freedom's advance or decline? *Affirmative!* Reflect on present trends—away from freedom and toward socialism—governmental interventionism. What has happened to prices? The dollar buys less and less as political know-it-all-ness takes over.

No one likes the result of this vandalism but few there are who relate the real cause to the plight so greatly deplored. Were the ever-increasing prices recognized as the result of this social error, there would be two intelligent decisions: (1) we'd resist omnipotent government and, (2) make a devoted effort to remove the cause by restoring government to the limited role our Founding Fathers prescribed. Pricing gives valuable instruction!

The nearest approach to our lofty goal had its inception in the Declaration, thanks to our Founding Fathers. Some years after its signing, that great English statesman, Edmund Burke, wrote that "it was a partnership between the living and the dead and the yet unborn." And how "the yet unborn" were graced by their noble efforts—some of us two centuries later being their partners. And proud of it!

It is now appropriate to identify the adversaries of our lofty goal—living the good life—and ask why they oppose. There are the millions who side with socialism, partially or entirely, many of whom would be offended to be so labeled. And there are more reasons than individuals for this intellectual delinquency. The explanation for this shiftless shifting?

Most people are not guided by a sound premise—a fundamental point of reference, their behaviors being in response to this or that petty urge. The reasons for socialistic nonsense are in the millions, so a few samplings must suffice.

Perhaps the most important reason is a failure correctly to interpret *self-interest*. This term is not included in any of my quotation books and the dictionary defines it as "selfishness; to one's own advantage at the expense of others." This tyranny of words causes nearly everyone to think of looking after self as sinning against all others—a societal crime. A great boon to mankind would be a general understanding of the real meaning of self-interest as set forth by William Graham Sumner: "Making the most of one's self . . . is not a separate thing from filling one's place in society, but *the two are one,* and the latter is accomplished when the former is done."

Most of these millions who believe that looking after self is a sin against others, advocate and participate in the greatest of all societal sins: *political thievery*. This is the robbing-Peter-to-pay-Paul way of life. They do untold damage to others as they "think" they help themselves. Result? Dictocrats in the driver's seat, inflation and so on—the road to enslavement.

Every act—no exception—which inhibits the free flow of creative action is part and parcel of this degradation. No need to enumerate the ways honest competition is disparaged and thwarted. Anyone who cannot readily recognize such hindrances to material, intellectual, moral and spiritual growth simply lacks the capacity to learn. And what a vast number that is!

A famous historian, John Neville Figgis, wrote: "Religious liberty is the residual legatee of religious quarrels." The terrible wars of the 16th and 17th centuries had been fought to the point of total exhaustion; there were no victors, only survivors. It began to dawn on a few thinkers on both sides that there was a better way to advance the faith: separate church and state and let people come to God in their own way. This idea is the first article in our own Bill of Rights.

What lesson does this teach us? *Forgo denunciation of today's socialists.* Don't lock horns with them. Let their nonsense run rampant! "Resist not evil"—give them nothing to scratch against. Leave them free to babble—free in their efforts to make carbon copies of their depraved selves. Their quarrels are the rope they'll hang themselves on, thereby allowing liberty to prevail.

For proof that this tactic is efficacious, merely note the turnabout in thinking presently under way. Ever so many, formerly indifferent or leaners toward socialism, are coming to themselves. Gas lines, all sorts of shortages, rapidly rising prices, inflation and countless other obstructions to the good life, are having a remarkable effect—an awakening!

Wrote Emerson: "Life is a series of surprises. We do not guess today the mood, the pleasure, the power of tomorrow, when we are building up our being." In other words, the future is uncertain. We build up our being in order to better cope with change. And essential for the building and subsequent adjustment is the freedom to choose and to act. Pleasant surprises? Beyond our power to imagine!

20

INFLUENCE: ITS ETERNAL RADIATION

Influence never dies; every act, emotion, look and word makes influence tell for good or evil, happiness or woe, through the long future of eternity.
—THOMAS à KEMPIS

Thomas à Kempis, the brilliant German monk (1380-1471) was not suggesting that a majority movement would lead to mankind's emergence. On the contrary, he referred to the influence each individual exerts.

Calvin Coolidge observed that "Men do not make laws. They do but discover them." Thomas à Kempis discovered a law of human action: every individual act—wise or stupid, good or bad—initiates an imperishable influence that goes on forever.

Here's how that law is described by a distinguished scientist, Donald Hatch Andrews:

If I wave my hand . . . it not only moves the leaves on the trees outside, creates ripples down on the water of the bay, but also moves the moon; the sun feels this motion, and the stars; even the farthest nebula will tremble because of the motion of my hand. As a famous physicist put it, every heartbeat is felt through the entire universe.

. . . there is in each of us an eternal core, call it dynamic force, call it personality, call it spirit or soul or symphony or what you will; there is in us this core, this director of our symphony of life that somehow has an invariance that transcends the changes of space and time. And in this way, we can understand that in mortal life there is this immortal reality that merges with the eternal.[1]

The universe is an integer, whether we move from large to small or small to large: There is no fraction so small that it is not divisible, and no number so large that it cannot be doubled.

The fact that every act and thought—be it good or bad—extends its influence not only in today's world but *forever* is, by and large, incomprehensible. Thus truth is foreign to—beyond the range of—day-to-day experiences, even normal imagination. Regretfully, a fantasy! Eternal radiation of our behaviors are thus "far-fetched," no less so than a wave of the hand radiates throughout the universe.

What a blessing to the future of mankind were a few of us to grasp the significance of today's intellectual, moral and spiritual example!

How comprehend the seemingly incomprehensible fact, that every action we take now reverberates throughout endless time? Merely reflect on how present parental be-

---

[1] See "The New Science and The New Faith" by Donald Hatch Andrews. *The Freeman*. April 1961.

havior influences the lives of their children. When parental example is bad, indecent, untidy, slovenly, the child, more than likely, will be a reflection thereof.

But not always! Thank goodness, there are bright-eyed youngsters who are not victimized by parental delinquency. They respond to the good example of authors or neighbors or teachers. The ones who really contribute to human advancement are parents and children who are attracted to and abide by righteousness—the seekers of truth!

To the German author, Jean Paul Richter (1763-1825), we are indebted for this profound thought: "The words that a father speaks to his children in the privacy of home are not heard by the world, but, as in whispering galleries, *they are clearly heard at the end, and by posterity.*" Whatever we do now goes on forever—shapes the future!

Is it not obvious that most individuals are unaware of having any influence beyond their immediate surroundings and their mortal moments? Blind to reality! Assume a general awakening among mankind to the fact that their behaviors today radiate eternally—the future of mankind deteriorating or improving as a consequence of present actions. What a glorious revolution this would be, another renaissance, responsibility restored to its rightful place, namely, on the shoulders of those graced with a discovery of how influence *can* work its wonders! Given this new sense of responsibility, men will act accordingly.

To this line of reasoning, many will respond that the millions who believe in socialism will wreak their damage on the future no less than those who begin a righteous way of life will confer their enlightenment. Wrong! The socialists among us have for several decades been doing all in their power to destroy the America that was. They have shot their bolt; they can do no more than they are doing now.

Out of the blue, so to speak, will bloom the new, enlightened and rewarding opposition causing the forces of socialism to fade into futility. Success, however, depends on consistency—no leaks, no "buts." And such consistency requires that devotees of freedom reason logically and deductively from a basic premise. That noted philosopher, Immanuel Kant (1724-1804), had a premise which he called "good will." By "will" he meant an ability to rationally will one's own actions. And the adjective "good" could be used only if the individual could apply the principle of universality to his maxims.

The meaning of that last line evaded me until I tested it on two simple maxims:

1—Do I have a right to my life, livelihood, liberty? Yes, that is good for I can concede that right to all human beings—universality!
2—Do I have the right to take the life, livelihood, liberty of another? Only if I can concede that same right to everyone else. Can I? No! Ergo, it is not good!

With the above guideline, one will never do anything which, if everyone did it, would bring on chaos—socialism and the like.

For proof that superb thoughts, writings, actions radiate today, tomorrow and forever, observe that we are blest with the works of the world's first civilization—the Sumerians.[2]

---

[2]See "Eruptions of Truth" in my book, *Awake for Freedom's Sake* (Irvington, N.Y.: The Foundation for Economic Education, Inc., 1977), pp. 22-29.

Influence: Its Eternal Radiation

The moral teachings of Confucius—25 centuries ago—enlighten us.

Move on five centuries to Jesus of Nazareth. Doubtless the greatest radiation of righteousness in all history!

We do not know the names of ever so many other contributors to peace on earth and good will toward men, but some are familiar. Just a few examples of exemplarity are Adam Smith, George Washington, Goethe, Edmund Burke, Bastiat, Emerson, Tennyson, Herbert Spencer, Lincoln, Ortega y Gasset, Edison, Kettering, Mises—on and on.

During the past fifty years I have become personally acquainted with many individuals in this and other nations whose works for freedom will radiate through the ages. Why am I writing this brevity on influence? Because the wisdom of Thomas à Kempis of five centuries ago radiates to me and others. To paraphrase Socrates:

Let him who would improve the world, first improve himself—*and thus serve eternity!*

21

FINDING ONE'S DUTY

Man is not born to solve the problems of the universe, but to find out what he has to do; and to restrain himself within the limits of his comprehension. —**GOETHE**

The late Robert A. Millikan, Chairman, Executive Council, California Institute of Technology, and a former FEE Trustee, corrected a common misunderstanding of duty when he wrote: "Duty has nothing to do with what somebody else conceives to be for the common good."

There are far more conceptions of what constitutes "the common good" than there are people. Why more? Each individual's assessment varies with every intellectual step he takes, backward or forward. Billions of changing perspectives! One's duty in life is never to be found by latching onto someone else's idea or notion of the common good; duty lies in another dimension.

And what might man's real dimension be? Goethe gave the correct answer: a human being must live "within the limits of his comprehension." Reflect on the difference between the infinite complexities of the universe and finite man's understanding. More fantastic than the difference between an atom and a galaxy!

Man is not born to solve the problems of the universe. Those who deny that there's anything in the universe intellectually above that tiny lump atop their shoulders are, they "think," the sole solvers of universal problems. Such is the affliction of ignorance, a fact now and then recognized as in these samplings.

> Ignorance deprives men of freedom because they do not know what alternatives there are. It is impossible to choose to do what one has "never heard of."
> —*Ralph Barton Perry*

> Better be unborn than untaught for ignorance is the root of misfortune. —*Plato*

> To be ignorant of one's ignorance is the malady of ignorance. —*Amos Bronson Alcott*

> It is impossible to make people understand their ignorance; for it requires knowledge to perceive it, and therefore he that can perceive it hath it not.
> —*Jeremy Taylor*

> By ignorance is pride increased; those most assume who know the least. —*John Gay*

The most bothersome, frustrating and destructive of all are the millions of dictocrats who make no attempt to solve the problems of the universe but who *sincerely* believe that it is their duty to solve your and my problems. Think of the countless problems each individual has and then attempt the impossible task of multiplying them by the total population. The problems? Here are a few: the kind of schooling we may have; minimum wages and maximum hours of work; what and with whom we may exchange; at what age and at what wage one may be employed; prices one may charge; on and on, from seat belts, to how many dogs one may own.

Why emphasize the sincerity of these people who would run our lives? Those who are unaware of how little they know lack any understanding that restrains know-it-all-ness. Thus blinded, they sincerely believe it is their duty to make others carbon copies of themselves. Nor do they see any wrong in using force to implement their untenable ambitions. Ridding ourselves of the burden of such blindness is the major societal problem of our time!

Find out what he has to do and to restrain himself within the limits of his comprehension. Why is this admonition rarely observed? An all too common fault among us is an unlimited appetite for attainment without a corresponding enthusiasm for the comprehension which must underlie that attainment. The only remedy is to grasp and abide by the law of cause and effect, explained so brilliantly by Emerson: "Cause and effect, means and ends, seed and fruit, *cannot be severed,* for the effect already blooms in the cause, the end pre-exists in the means, the fruit in the seed."

Briefly, most people not only wish for but believe they can have the fruits of life—enlightenment or prosperity or freedom or other rewarding desiderata—without planting any seeds. They pursue the idle day dream of something for nothing.

The enormous scale of the something-for-nothing syndrome, observed in all walks of life, accounts for our

Finding One's Duty

millions of dictocrats; it accounts for inflation and moral decline. Evil on the rampage! To reverse this decay is our problem—*our duty*. Hopeless? Just the opposite: hopeful! Wrote the American clergyman, E. H. Chapin (1814-80): "In the history of man it has been very generally the case, that when evils have become insufferable, they have reached the point of cure."

Have the evil consequences of socialism become insufferable? Yes, even socialists—the millions of Americans who believe in, advocate and practice one or more socialistic notions—vigorously complain about rising prices, inflation, gasoline and other shortages and so on. Insufferable evils even to the perpetrators thereof!

We have, indeed, reached "the point of cure." Now to the pertinent question: What *is* the cure? It is, like so many problems, as simple to state as it is difficult to achieve. The simple answer? *To restrain ourselves within the limits of our comprehension!* Why is this difficult? Because in the clear light of understanding, we must confess just how little we know, whereas in the darkness of ignorance we may pretend to know it all.

The antidote for know-it-all-ness—the root from which socialism grows—is an acute and abiding comprehension of how little we know. Such humility—a moral imperative—sets the stage for freedom. Standing in awe of all creation is the key to human creativity. So, how become aware of how little we know?

Here is the formula—simple as the ABCs! Visualize a sheet of black, *infinite* in dimensions. Now, assume that ten years ago I had achieved that measure of awareness, perception, consciousness symbolized by the small circle. A rather wise assessment of self! However, in the ensuing decade awareness has had a growth symbolized by the large circle. Merely note how much more darkness I am exposed to than, earlier. The more one knows the more is he aware of how little he knows! This is known as Socratic wisdom.

We Americans who would do our duty must learn from the past in order to overcome present mistakes and assure freedom for the future. This past, present and future sequence is remindful of a kindergarten maxim:

> Good, better, best;
> Never let it rest
> Until good becomes better
> And better becomes best.

Reflection brings enlightenment:

1—Our society was made *good* by the Declaration of Independence—unseating government as the endower of our rights and placing the Creator in that role.

Finding One's Duty

2—Our society was made *better* by the Constitution and the Bill of Rights—limiting government more appropriately than ever before in all history.

3—Our society became the *best* ever known by reason of the *good* and the *better*: a self-reliant citizenry!

No question about it, what happened two centuries ago was extraordinary. It was nothing less than an interception of Divine Providence on the part of a few, with resulting benefits for the many. Then, following a century of experiencing the blessings flowing from the freedom way, Americans have made a U-turn down the opposite road toward the planned economy and the welfare state: socialism.

It is beginning to dawn on me that this turnabout may be a blessing in disguise. Wrote the English poet, Edward Young: "How blessings brighten as they take their flight."

To a few, the blessings, as they recede, are becoming ever brighter. The likely result? There will be a renewal of interest in intercepting Divine Providence. There can be a return to what was once extraordinary only by extraordinary intellectual, moral and spiritual ascendancy on your and my part.

That our country may again be blest with freedom, let us be among those with unblemished hope. Wrote Alexander Pope:

Hope springs eternal in the human breast;
Man never is, but always to be blest.

22

SO HIGHLY ENDOWED

> *We hold these Truths to be self-evident, that all Men are created equal, that they are endowed by their Creator with certain unalienable Rights, that among these are Life, Liberty and the Pursuit of Happiness . . .*
> **—THE DECLARATION OF INDEPENDENCE, 1776**

I've sometimes wondered how differently we might have evolved had the Creator lavishly endowed us with property rather than the liberty to pursue happiness and to make the most of our lives in a world of scarce and limited resources. In such ponderings, I begin to understand the awful temptation of those possessing fewer wordly goods to envy the ones who have more. And I can better understand the caution of some wealthy individuals whose prime concern is to so protect their current holdings as to yield a comfortable life annuity.

So Highly Endowed

The more deeply I've reflected on such questions, the more it seems to me that the road to socialism may be strewn with endowments. In the preface to his play, *Knickerbocker Holiday,* the late Maxwell Anderson concluded that: "The guaranteed life turns out to be not only not free—it's not safe." His was one of the early warnings against the consequences of the Welfare State, consequences increasingly obvious in our more advanced "Age of Inflation."

To be a ward of the state can be a threat to the creative growth and upward evolution of the individual so sheltered, to say nothing of the untold harm to those otherwise productive persons taxed to provide such handouts. And the tendency is to drive such a society away from competitive private enterprise and freedom—toward socialism and slavery.

I'm reminded of a time several years ago when FEE faced serious financial difficulties. This was a matter of grave concern at an annual meeting of the Board of Trustees. One proposal the Trustees considered was to launch a fund drive to establish an endowment, the earnings or interest from which would be sufficient to cover the Foundation's operating expenses.

I argued vigorously against this proposal, contending that we of the FEE staff should face the daily challenge of performing well enough to earn our way—to attract financial support by our efforts, or to go out of business. It seemed to me that we needed such an incentive.

One of the Trustees then came to my rescue, citing an example he'd known of a church so highly endowed that the interest covered all expenses. The congregation had grown lax and indifferent, and the minister was preaching the gospel of socialism.

The point is that FEE was not then rescued by an endowment; we simply worked our way out of that financial difficulty, as we had done before and have done since. I do not pretend here a total indifference about our obligations to our suppliers or for the fulfillment of outstanding subscriptions. We try to maintain a reserve to cover contingencies. But a substantial endowment? Would we survive such a situation? I don't know.

For the sake of argument, let us stretch the imagination and assume that FEE's efforts had been so favorably received as to attract such funding. Suppose we did have a $10,000,000 reserve, relieving us of the financial pressure or incentive to meet a daily market demand.

What, in this circumstance, would be our incentive? Precisely the same as it was at the beginning—and always should be—*the love of freedom* for its own sake. Work on freedom's behalf regardless of obstacles—financial or otherwise!

Given this premise, how should we conduct ourselves? The only sensible answer: We should continue FEE's 34-year-old effort to generate an improved understanding and explanation of freedom. Let nothing stand in the way—regardless of how generous or skimpy the financial support. Our role as full-time workers is to serve as aides to all others whose aims parallel ours. It is research into this philosophy of freedom, refinement in the phrasing of this philosophy, bringing the wisdom of past and present to everyone who is interested. Briefly, our ambition is to become a good and faithful servant of The Creator, to aid in creation at the human level, to serve ourselves by serving you.

And what of your role? How best may you—having other and necessary occupations—participate in the greatest contest of all time—freedom versus socialism? There are ever so many ways. Among them:

1—Share your ideas with us. Hopefully, they may surpass our offerings, in which case we will share them with many thousands.
2—As for sharing such affluence as you possess, let your judgment and not ours be the guide. Large contributions make it possible to send all FEE material to nearly 50,000 individuals, all of whom are splendid workers in the vineyard but some of whom are unable to lend a hand financially.
3—Increasing financial assistance makes possible, (1) the expansion of our activities, (2) more gifts to educational institutions and (3) the pricing of our books, seminars and other services at an attractive level.
4—Whether or not you're in a position to lend a hand financially, remember that it is your deep interest in freedom that really matters.

We are fortunate to have been so highly endowed, not so much with property as with the liberty to make the most of our opportunities and our lives in free and open competition.

23

TOWARD THE IDEAL

Man can never come to his ideal standard. It is the nature of the immortal spirit to raise that standard higher and higher as it goes from strength to strength, still upward and onward. The wisest and greatest men are ever the most modest.

—MARGARET FULLER

Margaret Fuller (1810-50), according to my Encyclopedia "... was one of the most influential personalities of her day in American literary circles." It was Miss Fuller who translated into English Eckermann's *Conversations With Goethe,* one of the most interesting books I have ever read. Among the gems: "Nature understands no jesting. She is always true, always serious, always severe; she is always right, and the errors and faults are always those of man. The man incapable of appreciating her she despises, and only to

Toward the Ideal

the apt, the pure and the true, does she resign herself and reveal her secrets."

It is the wisest and greatest among us who are "the apt, the pure and the true." Thus qualified, they become aware that only as they increase their finite ability to intercept the revelations of Infinite Consciousness will Nature unlock her mysteries for them. This awareness is the source of modesty—the humble and the contrite heart.

Other persons—the vast majority—are blind to the fact that their bounties originate with Nature [God]. As a consequence, they ascribe their welfare to the political planners and bureaucrats who are blind as themselves—but claim omniscience. "Blind leaders of the blind." (Matthew 15:14)

It is this false self-assessment and misplaced confidence that, more than anything else, accounts for the world's woes throughout history and for our own slump into socialism. Is it any wonder that Nature despises and penalizes such arrogance!

Men can never come to the ideal standard. Why is the ideal never attained? It is not supposed to be! To illustrate: Assume that a carrot is the ideal eatable item of a mule. Hang it on a stick fastened to his neck and projected two feet in front of his mouth. Regardless of his anxious movement—slow or fast—he will never reach his eatable ideal.

The ideal is a Heavenly lodestar for the advancement of humanity. Were it ever attained all progress and emergence would be at an end. To concede the ideal's attainability is to deny the whole concept of Infinite Consciousness. If I may descend to the vernacular, the ideal is God's come-on.

It is the nature of the immortal spirit to raise that

standard higher and higher. It is otherwise with the above-mentioned mule. Noting no success in reaching that carrot, this mule—not the brightest of beasts—would soon abandon his eatable ideal.

The same can be said for ever so many freedom devotees. When the ideal for which we strive—the *perfect* society—is observed to be out of reach, they throw in the sponge—call it quits. They fail to recognize that this is the way it should be. Perfection is the unattainable goal—the intellectual, moral and spiritual lodestar. Wrote Chesterfield: "Aim at perfection in everything, though in *most* things it is unattainable. However, they who aim at it, and persevere, will come much nearer to it than those whose laziness and despondency make them give it up as unattainable."

The above is a wise guideline except I would omit "most." Samuel Johnson came nearer to this truth: "It is reasonable to have perfection in our eye that *we may always advance toward it, though we know it can never be attained.*"

From strength to strength. Wrote the Bard of Avon: "Oh! It is excellent to have a giant's strength; but it is tyrannous to use it like a giant." To grasp Shakespeare's observation, one must be aware of the two definitions of "giant." Says the dictionary: "a person of great intellect" and "a race of huge beings of human form who warred against the gods." The reference here is to the Titans of Greek mythology, who rebelled unsuccessfully against the Olympians and suffered dire punishments.

It is indeed excellent to have a mighty intellect, one that towers above the mill run of mankind. When those so blest adhere strictly to moral principles—the Golden Rule and the

Toward the Ideal 117

Ten Commandments—it is their leadership that resurrects—brings back to life—humanity from its countless falls. Our ambition should be to advance from today's strength, whatever its level, to a greater strength tomorrow.

However, it is ambition gone blind to flout reality and rebel against the very nature of things, to "war against the gods," as the Greeks put it. Tyranny is usurpation, a giant's strength put to destructive uses. Today in the U.S.A. we have millions of usurpers—political giants—putting their infamous brand of strength to the destruction of freedom.

These thoughts about "from strength to strength" were not original with Margaret Fuller. She merely knew of and understood an ancient wisdom recorded about 350 B.C.: "They [seekers of Truth] go from strength to strength till each appears before God." (Psalms 84:7) Such striving, she explained, is "the nature of the immortal spirit." Going in this direction is *progress* toward the immortal or Heavenly goal.

Let me share several thoughts by those who, relative to the rest of us, qualify as "the apt, the pure and the true."

- All growth [progress] that is not toward God [Infinite Consciousness] is growing in decay.
  —George Macdonald

- He that is good will infallibly become better, and he that is bad will as certainly become worse; for vice, virtue and time, are three things that never stand still.
  —Colton

- Every age has its problems, by solving which, humanity is helped forward.   *—Heinrich Heine*

- The individual and the race are always moving; and as

we drift [progress] into new latitudes new lights open in the heavens more immediately over us.
—*E. H. Chapin*

- If a man is not rising upward [progressing] to be an angel, depend upon it, he is sinking downward to be a devil. —*Coleridge*

- All our progress is an unfolding, like the vegetable bud. You have first an instinct, then an opinion, then a knowledge, as a plant has root, bud and fruit.
—*Emerson*

- Nature knows no pause in progress and development, and attaches her curse to all inaction. —*Goethe*

- We should so live and labor in our time that what came to us as seed may go to the next generation as blossom, and what came to us as blossom may go to them as fruit. This is what we mean by progress.
—*H. W. Beecher*

Let us progress toward the ideal—*FREEDOM*. Christian Bovee (1820-1904), an author and editor, phrased our ambition thus: "Intellectually, as well as politically, the direction of all true progress is toward greater freedom, and along an endless succession of ideas."

24

AS A MAN THINKETH

In every epoch of the world, the great events . . . is it not the arrival of a thinker?—**THOMAS CARLYLE**

This Scotsman (1795-1881), regardless of his intimate friendship with the Sage of Concord, was not of Emerson's or our faith. He believed in a strong paternalistic government! Further, his assessment of an "epoch" was far from the dictionary's definition: "The beginning of a new and important period in history." What was important to him is distressing to me. But we have been taught that "As a man thinketh in his heart so is he," and Carlyle's thinking was assuredly from the heart. And his statement, assuming one's ambition for a free society, is a gem! So here's something from my heart.

What a man thinketh is the genesis of progress of every kind, be it economic, intellectual, moral or spiritual. Here is how C. F. Kettering explained the genesis of human advancement: "Nothing ever built arose to touch the skies unless some man dreamed that it should, some man believed that it could, and some man willed that it must."

In 1934 Boss Ket wrote a brevity entitled *The Birth Of An Idea,* in which he reports that the radio had its beginning 2,500 years ago. "Thales of Miletus, found that by rubbing amber he produced a force that would pick up straws." Later, Queen Elizabeth's physician, Sir William Gilbert, did some more thinking and experimenting and called the phenomenon *electricity.*

Progress over the ages, a man here and there entertaining a new thought. Benjamin Franklin with his kite, and many others since his time, have contributed to the millions of wonders now being wrought by electrical energy!

That remarkable explanation by Kettering as to the genesis of human evolution assuredly was rooted in thoughts comparable to these, and the examples of each which follow:

> In *dreaming,* the soul doth often times foretell what is to come.   *—François Rabelais*

> In *belief* lies the secret of all possible exertions.
>   *—Bulwer-Lytton*

> The highest belief in the spiritual life is to be able always and in all things to say, "Not my will, but *thine* be done."
>   *—Tryon Edwards*

Leonardo da Vinci, more than five centuries ago, *dreamed* that some day man might fly like birds. He even designed and built a winged contraption but it couldn't get off the ground. Today? His dream has come to touch the sky—today's miraculous airplanes!

Alexander Graham Bell noted that the human voice could be transmitted about 50 yards at the speed of sound. He *believed* that the yardage and speed could be fantastically improved. In 1864 he invented the telephone, an instrument that converts the voice into electric impulses. Result? Around the earth in one-seventh of a second!

Perhaps no one can identify the man who first proclaimed "Thy *will* be done"—God's Will. Whoever that first man might have been, he was graced with an elevated thought, which was eventually responsible for that wisdom in the Declaration of Independence: "Men are endowed by their Creator with certain unalienable rights . . ." This unseated government as the endower of our rights to life and liberty and placed the Creator there—unquestionably the greatest step in politico-economic philosophy ever taken!

That heroic little band of men and women scattered over the centuries, who have dreamed and believed and willed, qualify as the initiators of human progress. They are the self-starters who have set the rest of us in motion. Among the millions times millions of innovations that have blest humanity is the self-starter on your automobile. Not only is this a good example to make the point here at issue but it recalls a vivid personal experience. Sixty-five years ago, when I was cranking by hand to start a 1912 Overland, the engine backfired breaking my wrist. It is easy to see why I have a deep appreciation for this remarkable product of those who think originally and aright.

The persons who think ahead are the self-starters who have set the rest of us in motion. Merely reflect on the hundreds of thousands of others who, beginning with Wilbur and Orville Wright, have made contributions to our present chariots of the air. Leonardo da Vinci had no more idea of what would result from his start than you or I have of what will grace the lives of our descendants 500 years hence—*assuming a return to freedom!*

Had a 747 jet flown over Leonardo's home, he would have thought the Heavens were falling. And he would not have been far wrong! Why this assertion? Most people believe that any new idea they experience has its origin in them. Not so! At best we can prepare our minds to receive an idea, but the idea itself is in the nature of an interception of Divine Omnipotence—Creation. To avoid the affliction of the Great I-Am, let us give credit where credit is due, namely, the Heavenly Source. From this Source, not only the self-starters but all others are privileged to draw.

Ever so many seekers of political office are among the great I-Ams. They actually "think" that we know not how to run our lives; but they never doubt that we are wise enough to select them as our masters! Confusion worse confounded! There may be a remedy for this double-barreled confusion by seeking the relationship between (1) giving credit where due and (2) charity.

True charity goes far beyond material gifts such as food or cash or other life-sustaining items. High in the realm of charity is the *giving of credit* to those millions who have made and are making our lives possible. It is, without question, others who give us opportunities, challenges, the road toward truth. Our debt to others is beyond our power to measure—an intellectual obligation we should never let go unpaid!

The problem is to rid ourselves of egotism—the I-am-it syndrome. Giving credit where it is due is the initial step—opening the door, as we say, to a new mental stance. Success depends on daily practice, a difficult discipline, for it requires the riddance of old habits. The enlightenments that hopefully may follow:

- Gone is the notion that I am the Source.
- Welcome is the good news, namely, that I am the beneficiary of thoughts, goods and services conferred by others.
- My new role is to serve others as they serve me—even better if possible.

Thank Heaven for the arrival, every now and then, of a freedom thinker. May each of us strive as best we can to be his ideological companion!

25

THE POWER OF TOMORROW

> *Life is a series of surprises. We do not guess today the mood, the pleasure, the power of tomorrow, when we are building up our being.* **—EMERSON**

When life is improving day-in-and-day-out, it will, regardless of one's endeavor, be filled with surprises. New moods and pleasures that cannot be foreseen today will grace our lives; every tomorrow will be freshly enriched. Is such a hopeful prognosis credible?

This brevity will be limited to a few comments on FEE's tomorrow. When we of the present Senior Staff no longer exist as working teammates—when we have passed on—what will be the fate of FEE? Will its work on behalf of the freedom way of life be at an end—passe!— and, if not, what are the possibilities of its being ever so much better than now? Briefly, what must we do now to assure a glorious tomorrow?

Evidence abounds that God—Creation, Infinite Consciousness—endows everyone with the *potential* virtue, temper, understanding, taste that lifts each life into that exalted role *we are ordained to fill*. Several thoughts that such a belief inspires:

- Most people are unaware of their potentialities. To use Carl Jung's term, each of us has a partner, "The Undiscovered Self."[1]
- Among those who are aware, ever so many fail to strive for discovery. Wealth, fame, notoriety, amusements and the like are higher ambitions!
- No two individuals have identical potentialities. Indeed, the intellectual gates are continually opening—changing, advancing—to those who are ardent seekers of Truth.
- All that is attained in the higher realms of life is *ordained* by Creation—no exception!

There is only one appropriate aim for those of us presently on the Senior Staff: to so conduct ourselves that we shall have *superior successors!* The Sage of Concord gave the only workable formula: *"When we are building up our beings."* He had this to say on another occasion: "God offers to every mind its choice between Truth and repose. Take which you please, you can never have both."

The ardent seeking of Truth and sharing one's findings with nary a deviation—no leaks or "buts"—with the few who may be interested must be our guideline. There can be no hankering for repose—hibernation—the all-too-common trait. Awake for freedom's sake!

---

[1] New American Library, A Mentor Book, 1958.

It is my fervent belief, based on 46 years of experience, that what happens Staff-wise and otherwise, is over and beyond our personal control. We are not in charge of the future. As related to our chosen endeavor, the future is determined by our *present* performances. If we are building up our individual beings—which to the best of our ability we are—what follows is ordained by a Source far over and beyond the human.

Time after time I have wondered who would succeed this or that excellent Staff member who retired or accepted a higher paying position. But experience has taught me to look upon that anxiety as inept. On every occasion, and as if by magic, superior individuals have put in an appearance. Never have I had associates to equal the present FEE staff, when it comes to understanding the freedom philosophy and dedication to its advancement.

The power of tomorrow, as related to human liberty, is determined by our power on its behalf today. *Let us not interfere or try to out-think the Great Ordainer.* Be assured of a series of surprises—pleasant and rewarding ones!

NAME INDEX

Acton, Lord, 26
Addison, Joseph, 15, 22
Alcott, Amos Bronson, 105
Amiel, Henri Frederic, 38
Anderson, Maxwell, 111
Andrews, Donald Hatch, 2, 99
Augustine (Saint), 51

Barzun, Jacques, 31
Bastiat, Frederic, 43
Beecher, H. W., 80, 118
Berrill, N. J., 71
Borah, Wm. Edgar, 11
Bovee, Christian, 118
Brooks, Phillips, 67, 94
Bryant, Wm. Cullen, 93
Bulwer-Lytton, Edw., 120
Burke, Edmund, 18, 62, 86, 96
Butler, Samuel, 35

Cabot, Richard, 70
Cameron, Margaret, 91
Carlyle, Thomas, 119
Carrel, Alexis, 3
Carver, Geo. Washington, 65
Chamfort, Sebastian, 11
Chapin, E. H., 107, 118
Chesterfield, Philip, 94, 116
Chesterton, G. K., 66
Clay, Henry, 29, 95
Coleridge, S. T., 92, 118
Colton, Caleb C., 69, 89, 117
Coolidge, Calvin, 99
Confucius, 16
Cowper, William, 23

Dickens, Charles, 59
Dillaway, Newton, 42
Dryden, John, 30

Edison, Thomas A., 76
Edwards, Tryon, 25, 29, 120
Emerson, Ralph Waldo, 42, 87, 98, 106, 118, 124
Epictetus, 53
Ezekiel, 24

Fenelon, François, 41
Fielding, Henry, 10
Figgis, John N., 98
Franklin, Benjamin, 62
Froude, J. A., 10, 75
Fuller, Margaret, 114
Fuller, Richard, 33
Fuller, Thomas, 91

Gay, John, 22, 105
Gibbon, Edward, 22
Goethe, 9, 23, 58, 62, 104, 118
Guthrie, Thomas, 1

Halifax, Lord, 91
Hall, Verna, 66
Hazlitt, Wm., 22, 50
Heine, Heinrich, 117
Hocking, Wm. Ernest, 66
Home, Henry, 23
Horace, 3, 26
Howells, Wm. Dean, 41

James, 7
John, 20, 93

Johnson, Samuel, 116
Jowett, Benjamin, 46
Jung, Carl, 125

Kant, Immanuel, 48, 102
Kempis, Thomas à, 51, 99
Kettering, C. F., 79, 119
Kingsley, Charles, 52
Kunkel, Fritz, 12, 74

La Bruyère, Jean de, 21
Landor, W. S., 95
Lavater, J. K., 59
Lewis, C. S., 6, 69
Lincoln, Abraham, 45, 67
Longfellow, H. W., 55, 80

Macdonald, George, 117
Mackay, Charles, 12
Michelangelo, 69
Millikan, Robert A., 104
Mises, Ludwig von, 14
Montaigne, Michel, 39, 88

Newton, Isaac, 89

Opitz, E. A., 72

Perry, Ralph Barton, 105
Plato, 3, 37, 105
Plutarch, 7
Pope, Alexander, 109

Quarles, Francis, 63

Rabelais, François, 120
Richter, Jean Paul, 101
Rogge, Benjamin, 15
Rolston, Holmes, III, 56
Russell, P. Dean, 16

Santayana, George, 15
Shakespeare, 116
Smith, Adam, 1
Socrates, 87
South, Robert, 76
Spencer, Herbert, 33
Stamp, Josiah, 64
Story, Joseph, 92
Sumner, Wm. Graham, 23, 97

Talleyrand, 85
Taylor, Jeremy, 105
Terence, 91
Thoreau, Henry D., 62
Tillotson, John, 32
Tocqueville, Alexis de, 77

Voltaire, 60, 91

Washington, Booker T., 65
Washington, George, 14, 40
Webster, Daniel, 67
Wilcox, Carlos, 62
Wordsworth, Wm., 44, 59

Young, Edward, 109